The *Natural Histories* of Pliny the Elder

The *Natural Histories* of Pliny the Elder

An Advanced Reader and Grammar Review

P. L. CHAMBERS

UNIVERSITY OF OKLAHOMA PRESS : NORMAN

Also by P. L. Chambers

Latin Alive and Well: An Introductory Text (Norman, 2007)
The Attic Nights *of Aulus Gellius: An Intermediate Reader and Grammar Review* (Norman, 2009)

Library of Congress Cataloging-in-Publication Data

Chambers, P. L. (Peggy L.)
The natural histories of Pliny the Elder : an advanced reader and grammar review / P. L. Chambers.
p. cm.
ISBN 978-0-8061-4215-9 (pbk. : alk. paper)
1. Pliny, the Elder. Naturalis historia. 2. Pliny, the Elder—Language. 3. Latin language—Grammar. 4. Natural history—Pre-Linnean works. I. Pliny, the Elder. II. Title.
PA6637.C47 2012
508—dc23
2011012387

The paper in this book meets the guidelines for permanence and durability of the Committee on Production Guidelines for Book Longevity of the Council on Library Resources, Inc. ∞

1 2 3 4 5 6 7 8 9 10

Contents

Preface

Gaius Plinius Secundus (23–79) is best known today as Pliny the Elder to distinguish him from his nephew and adoptive son, Pliny the Younger. His ancestral home was in and around Como in Transpadane Gaul (northern Italy). He was of equestrian rank and served in the military in Germany under the command of Drusus Nero. This was followed by administrative posts in Gaul and Spain under the emperor Vespasian. He ultimately became prefect of the fleet in Misenum. It was here in the Bay of Naples that he met his death in the eruption of Vesuvius in A.D. 79, an event immortalized by Pliny the Younger in correspondence with the historian Tacitus.

In the intervals of an extremely active public career, Pliny the Elder wrote on a prodigious scale. Pliny the Younger outlines the impressive number of his uncle's works as well as his astounding work schedule in the letter that follows.

> Gaius Plinius Sends Greetings to Baebius Macer
> I am delighted to hear that your close study of my uncle's books has made you wish to possess them all. Since you ask me for a complete list, I will provide a bibliography, and arrange it in chronological order, for this is the sort of information likely to please scholars.
>
> *Throwing the Javelin from Horseback*—one volume; a work of industry and talent written when he was a junior officer in the cavalry.
>
> *The Life of Pomponius Secundus*—two volumes. My uncle was greatly loved by him and felt he owed this as an act of homage to his friend's memory.
>
> *The German Wars*—twenty volumes, covering all the wars we have ever had with the Germans. He began this during his military service in Germany, as the result of a dream; in his sleep he saw standing over him the ghost of Drusus Nero, who had triumphed far and wide in Germany and died there. He committed his memory to my uncle's care, begging him to save him from the injustice of oblivion.
>
> *The Scholar*—three volumes divided into six sections on account of their length, in which he trains the orator from his cradle and brings him to perfection.
>
> *A Continuation of the History of Aufidius Bassus*—thirty-one volumes.
>
> *A Natural History*—thirty-seven volumes, a learned and comprehensive work as full of variety as nature itself.
>
> You may wonder how such a busy man was able to complete so many volumes, many of them involving detailed study; and wonder still more when you learn that up to a certain age he practiced at the bar, that he died at the age of fifty-five, and throughout the intervening years his time was much taken up with the important offices he held and his friendship with the emperors. But he combined a penetrating intellect with amazing powers of concentration and the capacity to manage with the minimum of sleep.

From the feast of Vulcan onward he began to work by lamplight, not with any idea of making a propitious start but to give himself more time for study, and would rise halfway through the night; in winter it would often be at midnight or an hour later, and two at the latest. Admittedly he fell asleep very easily, and would often doze and wake up again during his work. Before daybreak he would visit the Emperor Vespasian (who also made use of his nights) and then go to attend his official duties. On returning home, he devoted any spare time to his work. After something to eat (his meals during the day were light and simple in the old-fashioned way), in summer when he was not too busy he would often lie in the sun, and a book was read aloud while he made notes and extracts. He made extracts of everything he read, and always said that there was no book so bad that some good could not be got out of it. After his rest in the sun he generally took a cold bath, and then ate something and had a short sleep; after which he worked till dinner time as if he had started on a new day. A book was read aloud during the meal and he took rapid notes. I remember that one of his friends told a reader to go back and repeat a word he had mispronounced. "Couldn't you understand him?" said my uncle. His friend admitted that he could. "Then why make him go back? Your interruption has lost us at least ten lines." To such lengths did he carry his passion for saving time. In summer he rose from dinner while it was still light, in winter as soon as darkness fell, as if some law compelled him.

This was his routine in the midst of his public duties and the bustle of the city. In the country, the only time he took from his work was for his bath, and by bath I mean his actual immersion, for while he was being rubbed down and dried he had a book read to him or dictated notes. When traveling he felt free from other responsibilities to give every minute to work; he kept a secretary at his side with book and notebook, and in winter saw that his hands were protected by long sleeves, so that even bitter weather should not rob him of a working hour. For the same reason, too, he used to be carried about Rome in a chair. I can remember how he scolded me for walking; according to him I need not have wasted those hours, for he thought any time wasted which was not devoted to work. It was this application which enabled him to finish all those volumes, and to leave me 160 notebooks of selected passages, written in a minute hand on both sides of the page, so that their number is really doubled. He used to say that when he was serving as procurator in Spain he could have sold these notebooks to Larcius Licinus for 400,000 sesterces, and there were far fewer of them then.

When you consider the extent of his reading and writing I wonder if you feel that he could never have been a public official nor a friend of the emperor, but on the other hand, now that you know of his application, that he should have achieved more? In fact his official duties put every possible obstacle in his path; and yet there was nothing which his energy could not surmount. So I cannot help smiling when anyone calls me studious, for compared with him I am the idlest of men. But am I the only one, seeing that so much of my time is taken up with official work and service to my friends? Any one of your lifelong devotees of literature, if put alongside my uncle, would blush to feel themselves thus enslaved to sleep and idleness.

I have let my letter run on, though I intended only to answer your question about the books left by my uncle. However, I feel sure that reading these details will give you as much pleasure as the actual books, and may even spur you on to the ambition of doing more than read them, if you can produce something similar yourself. Vale.

(C. Plinii Caecilii Secundi Epistularum, Bk III, v)

The *Natural Histories*, dedicated to Titus in A.D. 77, is by far Pliny the Elder's most ambitious work, listing more than four thousand authors as sources. It represents a survey of the knowledge of the natural world as seen by an educated Roman of the first century. The broad topics of the original work include cosmology and astronomy, geography, biology, zoology, botany, medicine, and finally metals, minerals, and precious stones. From among these I have chosen excerpts for translation that I have found entertaining, enlightening, and revealing of Roman thought, character, philosophy, and prejudice.

A Note to the Student

Reading the original works of Latin authors is challenging. To translate material concerning topics and events of two thousand years ago in a language with no linear syntax requires that the student be cognizant of a seemingly overwhelming array of grammatical points. And before you can begin translating, you must spend an immense amount of time looking up new vocabulary. I have experienced these problems, both as a student and as a teacher. Because I think Latin authors have relevance for our current world and can be enjoyable reading, I have written a series of texts devised to enable you to translate Latin authors in a minimum of time. The method I employ in each of my readers is as follows.

1. *Referenced quick grammar review*. Every chapter begins with a list of specific grammatical forms you will encounter in the chapter. To help you review them quickly, I have referenced each form to a "Compiled Grammar Charts" section at the back of the book. If there is no page number listed for a grammar review topic, it is because the topic cannot be listed in a table format. A review will be attained automatically through the assignments in the chapter as the exercises and sentences are designed to make these topics familiar before encountering them in the translation at hand. Also, you can access unreferenced topics online or in any introductory text.

2. *Pertinent explanations of new grammar.* Rather than list theoretical explanations, I use examples from the chapter at hand to demonstrate specific grammatical points not covered in most introductory courses.

3. *Sentences*. To ease translation and reduce frustration, I have devised sentences based on the original text. After translating these sentences, you will know the basic outline of the story and be able to identify grammatical forms and syntax in the original text.

4. *Particular vocabulary list for the translation at hand.* To enable you to devote more time to translating and to save you the frustration of looking up every new word in a dictionary (which lists multiple translation possibilities), I have put together a vocabulary list for each chapter that is specific to the chapter reading. To keep this list as brief as possible, I have omitted common words covered in most introductory texts. Vocabulary that appears in most introductory courses is in the glossary at the back of the book.

5. *NB* (*Nota Bene)*. NB, literally "Take note," is a Latin abbreviation used to denote that special attention should be paid to something. I use NB to point out aids for you in using this text and in making translations and to bring to your attention common introductory Latin words that in the reading at hand have different and specific meanings.

A Note to the Teacher

The Natural Histories *of Pliny the Elder* is a combination reader and grammar review. Each chapter begins with a listing of basic grammar that will be encountered in the translation at hand. I reference this grammar to the "Compiled Grammar Charts" at the back of the text. If there is no page number listed for a grammar review topic, it is because this topic cannot be listed in a table format. These are topics covered in most introductory courses. The exercises and sentences are designed to review and make familiar these topics before the student encounters them in the translation at hand. For this reason, I always go over these topics before making any chapter assignment. After the student has encountered the same grammatical form several times, I no longer list it for review. Grammatical forms and vocabulary not covered in most introductory courses are identified and explained in each chapter as they occur. The vocabulary list accompanying each chapter is provided only for reference and assistance in translation. The student is not expected to memorize this list, though certainly by the end of the course she or he will have become familiar with words favored by Pliny the Elder. The glossary at the end of the book covers the basic vocabulary that characterizes almost every introductory text. I have noted with NB common introductory Latin words that in the reading at hand have different and specific meanings.

To facilitate translation, I have devised sentences based on the text translation. These acquaint the student with the subject and basic outline of the passage before she or he encounters the original text. As you progress through the text, some particular chapters will not have sentences. This is because the student will have become more familiar with grammar and will be able to read these particular translations without any assistance with syntax. The text translations consist of entire texts or excerpts from the lines and books listed in the contents. These translations represent the original manuscript. I use ellipses (. . .) to denote omissions from the original.

The Natural Histories *of Pliny the Elder* is part of a series of coordinated texts designed to enable students as quickly as possible to read in the original language the authors of our Greco-Roman heritage. The other texts in my series are *Latin Alive and Well: An Introductory Text* and *The* Attic Nights *of Aulus Gellius: An Intermediate Reader and Grammar Review.*

The method I employ has proved highly successful in the classroom and is popular with students.

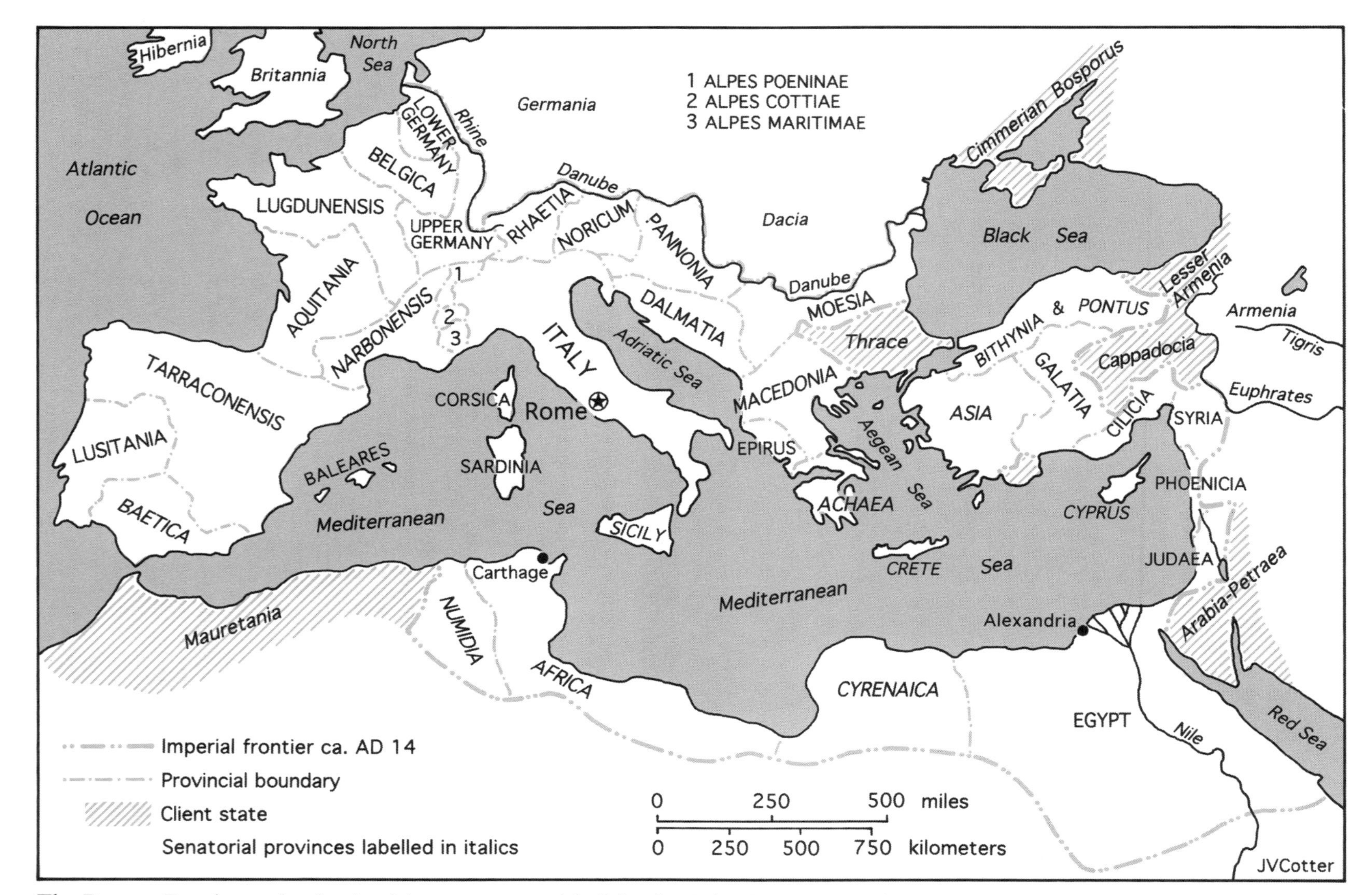

The Roman Empire at the death of Augustus, A.D. 14. (Map by John Cotter, reproduced courtesy of Paul A. Zoch)

The *Natural Histories* of Pliny the Elder

Geography of the World

I

Grammar Review

Alternate 3rd-Person Plural Perfect Active Indicative Forms	p. 127
Compiled Chart of Major Ablative Usages	p. 149
Compiled Chart of Adverb Formation	p. 148
Compiled Chart of Regular Comparative and Superlative Adjectives	p. 148
ipse, ipsa, ipsum	p. 144
Participles of Regular Verbs	
Cardinal and Ordinal Numbers	
Partitive Genitives	

New Grammar

donec (until) is used with the subjunctive to denote expectancy.

> Proxima Africae incolitur Aegyptus, introrsus ad meridiem recedens
> ***donec*** *a tergo praetendantur Aethiopes.*

> Next to Africa is inhabited Egypt, receding inward to the south
> **until** from the rear the Ethiopians are bordered.

Roman numerals

An overline over a Roman numeral indicates a multiplier of 1,000.

I = 1	XL = 40	DC = 600
IV = 4	L = 50	CM = 900
V = 5	LX = 60	M = 1,000
VI = 6	XC = 90	$\overline{V}$ = 5,000
IX = 9	C = 100	$\overline{X}$ = 10,000
X = 10	CCX = 210	$\overline{C}$ = 100,000
XI = 11	D = 500	$\overline{M}$ = 1,000,000

Roman measures of length and distance

passus,-us m., pace, a Roman measure of length consisting of five Roman feet
mille passus (1,000 paces) a mile
$\overline{\text{CLXX}}$ **passuum* 170 miles
* Numbers of more than 1,000 require the partitive genitive.

NB:		
	ab + abl.	from/because of
	a tergo	from the rear
	*fec**ere***	*fec**erunt***
	longe	adv., by far
	quā	adv., where
	tantum	adv., only
	vel maxime	adv., especially

Sentences

1. Universus orbis terrarum in tres partes dividitur—Europam, Asiam, et Africam.
2. Graeci Africam, Libyam, et mare ante Libyam, Libycum mare appellaverunt.
3. Libya finitur Aegypto; nec alia pars terrarum pauciores sinus ab occidente obliquo spatio litorum recipit.
4. Nomina populorum Libyae et nomina oppidorum vel maxime ineffabilia sunt, praeterquam linguis ipsorum.
5. Aegyptus proximam partem Africae incolit, et recedens introrsus ad meridiem donec Aethiopes a tergo praetendantur.
6. Nilus inferiorem partem eius dextera in laevaque determinat, divisus suo amplexu.

Translation

. . . Terrarum orbis universus in tres dividitur partes, Europam Asiam Africam. Origo ab occasu solis et Gaditano freto, quā inrumpens oceanus Atlanticus in maria interiora diffunditur. Hinc intranti dextera Africa est, laeva Europa, inter has Asia; termini amnes Tanais et Nilus.

. . . Primum ergo de Europa altrice victoris omnium gentium populi (5) longeque terrarum pulcherrima, quam plerique merito non tertiam portionem fecere verum aequam, in duas partes ab amne Tanai ad Gaditanum fretum universo orbe diviso.

. . . Africam Graeci Libyam appellavere et mare ante eam Libycum. Aegypto finitur; nec alia pars terrarum pauciores recipit sinus longe ab (10) occidente litorum obliquo spatio. Populorum eius oppidorumque nomina vel maxime sunt ineffabilia praeterquam ipsorum linguis; et alias castella ferme inhabitant.

. . . Proxima Africae incolitur Aegyptus, introrsus ad meridiem recedens donec a tergo praetendantur Aethiopes. Inferiorem eius partem Nilus dextera (15) laevaque divisus amplexu suo determinat, Canopico ostio ab Africa, ab Asia Pelusiaco, $\overline{\text{CLXX}}$ passuum intervallo.

Vocabulary

Aegyptus,-i f., Egypt
Aethiops,-opis Ethiopian
Africa,-ae f., Africa
alias adv., otherwise/apart from this
altrix,-icis f., foster mother
amnis,-is m., river
amplexus,-us m., encircling/surrounding
Atlanticus,-a,-um Atlantic
Canopicus,-,a,-um Canopic/of the town of Canopus, west of the Nile
castellum,-i n., fortress/refuge
determino (1) to bound/determine

dexter,dextera,dexterum right/on the right
diffundo,diffundere,diffudi, diffusum to spread out
divido,dividere,dividi,divisum to separate/divide
donec conj., until/up to the point at which
Europa,-ae f., Europe
ferme adv., mainly/for the most part
finio,finire,finivi,finitum to bound/limit
fretum,-i n., strait/channel
Gaditanus,-a,-um of Gades/modern city of Cádiz
hinc adv., here
incolo,incolere,incolui to inhabit/occupy
ineffabilis,-e unpronounceable
inferus,-a,-um low
inhabito (1) to inhabit/dwell
inrumpo,-rumpere,-rupi,-ruptum to burst
interior,interius comp. adj., interior/inner
intervallum,-i n., interval/intervening space
intro (1) to enter
introrsus adv., inward/inwardly
laeva,-a,-um left
Libya,-ae f., Libya
Libycus,-a,-um Libyan
lingua,-ae f., language/tongue
meridies,-ei m., the south
merito + dat. adv., deservedly/with good reason
Nilus,-i m., Nile River
obliquus,-a,-um slanting/oblique
occasus,-us m., the setting (sun)
occidens,-ntis western
oceanus,-i m., the ocean
oppidum,-i n., town
orbis terrae, orbis terrarum m., the world
origo,originis f., beginning/starting
ostium,-i n., mouth
passus,-us m., pace/step
Pelusiacus,-a,-um Pelusiac/of the Egyptian city Pelusium
plerusque,pleraque,plerumque very many
portio,-onis f., part/portion
praetendo,-tendere,-tendi,-tentum to stretch out/ border
praeterquam adv., except
primum adv., first
proximus,-a,-um next
recedo,-cedere,-cessi,-cessum to go back/recede
sinus,-us m., bay
sol,solis m., sun
spatium,-i n., extent/line
Tanais,-is m., the Don River
tantum adv., only
terminus,-i m., boundary
universus,-a,-um whole/entire
vel maxime adv., especially
verum adv., but in truth
victor,-oris adj., triumphant/victorious

The Nile and Alexandria

II

Grammar Review

Alternate 3rd-Person Plural Perfect Active Indicative Forms	p. 127
Deponent Verbs	p. 135
Gerunds	p. 131
Irregular Comparative Superlative Adjectives and Adverbs	p. 148
Partitive Genitives	

New Grammar

Declension pattern of 3rd-declension Greek adjectives.

Nom.	*Nilotis*	= adj., of/relating to the Nile River
Gen.	*Nilidis*	
Dat.	*Nilidi*	
Acc.	*Niliden*	
Abl.	*Nilide*	

Jussive subjunctives may be used to express duty or obligation and are then translated as "should" or "must."

Iure Alexandria ***laudetur***.

1. Rightly Alexandria **should/must be praised**.

Overlines over Roman numerals indicate a multiplier of a thousand.

C = 100 $\overline{\text{C}}$ = 100,000

Roman distance is expressed in paces (*passus,-us* = m., pace/step).

mille passus (1,000 paces), a Roman mile, is often abbreviated "p."

$\overline{\text{V}}$ p. = 5 miles (5,000 paces)

Originally the accusative singular of 3rd-declension masculine and feminine *i*-stem nouns and adjectives ending in ***–im***, the ablative singular in ***–i***, the accusative plural in ***–is***.

Nom.	Mareotis = f., Lake Mareotis
Gen.	Mareotis
Dat.	Mareoti
Acc.	Mareot**im**
Abl.	Mareot**i**

	singular		plural	
	m./f.	n.	m./f.	n.
Nom.	omnis	omne	omnes	omnia
Gen.	omnis		omnium	
Dat.	omni		omnibus	
Acc.	omn**im**	omne	omn**is**	omnia
Abl.	omn**i**		omnibus	

NB: *invenere* = *invenerunt*

Sentences

1. Nilus incertis fontibus oritur ut per ardentia deserta inmenso spatio longitudinis ambulat.
2. Habet originem, ut rex Iuba potuit exquirere in monte inferioris Mauretaniae non procul oceano in lacu protinus stagnante; hunc lacum Niliden vocant.
3. Ibi pisces reperiuntur: alabetae, coracini, siluri et quoque crocodili; inde ob argumentum crocodilus dicatus a Iuba in Iseo Caesareae potest spectari hodie.
4. Cum Nilus crescit, iudicatum est nefas reges aut praefectos navigare eo.
5. Iure Alexandria, condita a Magno Alexandro, laudetur. Est in litore Aegyptii aris in Africae parte $\overline{XII}$ p. ab ostio Canopico iuxta lacum Mareotim qui locus antea Rhacotes nominabatur.
6. Dinochares architectus metatus est Alexandriam laxitate $\overline{XV}$ p. insessa ad effigiem Macedonicae chlamydis.

Chapter II

Translation

Nilus incertis ortus fontibus, ut per deserta et ardentia et inmenso longitudinis spatio ambulans famaque tantum inermi quaesitus sine bellis quae ceteras omnis terras invenere, originem, ut Iuba rex potuit exquirere, in monte inferioris Mauretaniae non procul oceano habet lacu protinus stagnante, quem vocant Niliden. Ibi pisces reperiuntur alabetae, coracini, siluri; crocodilus quoque inde ob argumentum hoc Caesareae in Iseo dicatus ab eo spectatur hodie. Praeterea observatum est, prout in Mauretania nives imbresve satiaverint, ita Nilum increscere.

. . . Cum crescit, reges aut praefectos navigare eo nefas iudicatum est. Auctus per puteos mensurae notis deprehenduntur. Iustum incrementum est cubitorum XVI. Minores aquae non omnia rigant, ampliores detinent tardius recedendo; hae serendi tempora absumunt solo madente, illae non dant sitiente. . . .

Sed iure laudetur in litore Aegyptii maris Alexandria a Magno Alexandro condita in Africae parte ab ostio Canopico $\overline{\text{XII}}$ p. iuxta Mareotim lacum, qui locus antea Rhacotes nominabatur. Metatus est eam Dinochares architectus pluribus modis memorabili ingenio, $\overline{\text{XV}}$ p. laxitate insessa ad effigiem Macedonicae chlamydis orbe gyrato laciniosam, dextra laevaque anguloso procursu, iam tum tamen quinta situs parte regiae dicata. . . .

Vocabulary

absumo,-sumere,-sumpsi,-sumptum to use up/ consume
Aegyptius,-a,-um Egyptian
Africa,-ae f., Africa
alabetes,-ae m., alabeta, a fish common in the Nile
Alexander,-dri m., Alexander the Great
Alexandria,-ae f., city founded by Alexander the Great
ambulo,ambulare to proceed
amplus,-a,-um great/ample
angulosus,-a,-um angular
antea adv., formerly
aqua,-ae f., water
architectus,-i m., architect
ardens,-entis scorching/fiery
argumentum,-i proof/piece of evidence
auctus,-us m., rise
Caesarea,-ae f., the Palestinian coastal town built by Herod the Great and dedicated to Augustus, eventually became the administrative capital of Judea
Canopicus,-a,-um of the town of Canopus, on the western mouth of the Nile
chlamys,-ydis f., soldier's cape
condo,condere,condidi,conditum to found
coracinus,-i m., a dark-colored species of fish found in the Nile River
cresco,crescere,crevi,cretum to rise
crocodilus,-i m., crocodile
cubitum,-i n., cubit (1½ feet)
deprehendo,-hendere,-hendi,-hensum to detect
deserta,-orum n. pl., desert/wilderness
detineo,-tinere,-tenui,-tentum to delay the start of (agriculture)
dexter,-tra,-trum right
dico (1) to dedicate
Dinochares,-is m., architect appointed by Alexander to lay out Alexandria in Egypt
effigies,-ei f., shape/likeness
exquiro,-quirere,-quisivi,-quisitum to seek out/ ascertain
fons,fontis m., spring/source
gyratus,-a,-um rounded
hodie adv., today
imber,-bris m., rain
incrementum,-i n., rise/increase
incresco,increscere,increvi to increase (in volume)/rise
inermis,-e peaceful (explorer)
inferus,-a,-um low
ingenium,-i n., ability
inmensus,-a,-um immense/vast
insido,-sidere,-sedi,-sessum to merge
Iseon,-i n., Temple of Isis
Iuba,-ae m., the king of Mauretania celebrated for his learning, appointed by Augustus
iudico (1) to judge/decide
iure adv., rightly
iustus,-a,-um average/right
iuxta + acc. near/close to
laciniosus,-a,-um indented
lacus,-us m., lake
laevus,-a,-um left
laxitas,-atis f., area
litus,litoris n., coast/shore
longitudo,-inis f., length
Macedonicus,-a,-um Macedonian
madeo,madere,madui,maditum to be wet/soaked
Mareotis,-is f., Lake Mareotis near Alexandria
Mauretania,-ae f., a country of North Africa formed into two provinces by Claudius
memorabilis,-e remarkable
mensura,-ae f., standard measure/scale
metor,metari to lay out
mons,montis m., mountain
navigo (1) to travel (by water)/sail
nefas indecl., not right/wrong/contrary to divine command
Nilotis,Nilidis adj., of/relating to the Nile
Nilus,-i m., the Nile River
nix,nivis f., snow
nomino (1) to call/name
nota,-ae f., mark/note
ob + acc. for (the purpose of)
observo (1) to observe/regard
oceanus,-i m., ocean
orbis,-is m., circumference
origo,-inis f., origin/source
orior,oriri,ortus sum to arise
ostium,-i n., mouth (of a river)
piscis,-is m., a fish
praefectus,-i m., ruler/officer
praeterea further more
procul adv., far
procursus,-us m., projection
protinus adv., immediately
prout (pro. + ut) conj., in proportion as/in accordance as

puteus,-i m., a well
recedo,-cedere,-cessi,-cessum to recede
regia,-ae f., palace
Rhacotes,-is f., Rhacotes, the ancient city near the Nile River
rigo (1) to irrigate/moisten
satio (1) to be excessive/overfill
securitas,-atis f., security
sero,serere,sevi,satum to sow/plant
silurus,-i m., silurus, an unidentified Nile fish
sitio,sitire,sitivi,sititum to be parched
situs,-us m., site
solum,-i n., soil
spatium,-i n., extent
specto (1) to view/see
stagno (1) to pool/form a pool
tarde adv., slowly

Syria, Judaea, the Jordan, and the Dead Sea

Grammar Review

idem,eadem,idem p. 146

New Grammar

Declension pattern of 3rd-declension Greek nouns ending in *-e,-es*

Nom.	*Palaestine*	f., Palestine
Gen.	*Palaestines*	
Dat.	*Palaestinae*	
Acc.	*Palaestinen*	
Abl.	*Palaestine*	

Ablatives of comparison occur with comparatives and are translated as *than.*

*Iope Phoenicum antiquior terrarum **inundatione.***

Phoenician Joppa more ancient **than the inundation** of the world.

Ablatives of respect occur without a preposition and denote in respect to what something is or is done. *fessus **vita*** = weary/tired **in respect to life**

Supines are formed by converting the 4th principal part of verbs into a 4th-declension noun. The **ablative singular of the supine** is translated as an infinitive: *Incredibilis **dictu**.* = Incredible **to say**.

NB:			
	ab + abl.		on
	fuere	=	*fuerunt*
	idem,eadem,idem		the same as/identical with
	inde		adv, next
	in diem		day by day/daily
	longe lateque		far and wide
	maxumus,-a,-um	=	*maximus,-a,-um*
	per + acc.		along
	quā		adv, where
	quo		adv, conj., in consequence of which
	usque quā		to the extent that/as far as

Sentences

1. Iuxta Syria quondam maxuma terrarum et distincta plurimis nominibus occupat litus. Mox Idumaea incipit et Palaestine; regio per oram Samaria; tum Iope Phoenicum.

2. Inde Apollonia et Stratonis turris, quae est eadem Caesarea condita ab rege Herode, nunc colonia Prima Flavia deducta ab imperatore Vespasiano. Haec est finis Palaestines CLXXXIX passuum a confinio Arabiae.

3. Pars Iudaeae iuncta Syriae vocatur Galilaea, vero pars proxima Arabiae et Aegypto vocabatur Peraea. Peraea asperis montibus dispersa est et Iordane amne ab ceteris Iudaeis discreta est. Hic amnis amoenus Asphaltiten influit. Asphaltites gignit nihil praeter bitumen, unde nomen Graecum dabatur.

4. Ab occidente Asphaltitis sunt Esseni qui fugiunt litora usque qua nocent. Haec est gens sola et mira praeter ceteras gentes in toto orbe, sine ulla femina, omni venere abdicata, sine pecunia.

Translation

Iuxta Syria litus occupat, quondam terrarum maxuma et plurimis distincta nominibus: namque Palaestine vocabatur quā contigit Arabas, et Iudaea, et Coele, exin Phoenice, et quā recedit intus Damascena. . . .

. . . Mox Idumaea incipt et Palestine . . . Regio per oram Samaria; Iope Phoenicum antiquior terrarum inundatione, ut ferunt, insidet collem praeiacente saxo in quo vinculorum Andromedae vestigia ostendunt. Inde Apollonia, Stratonis turris, eadem Caesarea, ab Herode rege condita, nunc colonia Prima Flavia a Vespasiano imperatore deducta, finis Palaestines $\overline{\text{CLXXXIX}}$ p. a confinio Arabiae . . .

Supra Idumeam et Samariam Iudaea longe lateque funditur. Pars eius Syriae iuncta Galilaea vocatur, Arabiae vero et Aegypto proxima Peraea, asperis dispersa montibus et a ceteris Iudaeis Iordane amne discreta. Reliqua Iudaea dividitur in toparchias decem quo dicemus ordine: Hiericuntem palmetis consitam, fontibus riguam, Emmaum, Lyddam, Iopicam, Acrebitenam, Gophaniticam, Thamniticam, Bethleptephenen, Orinen, in qua fuere Hierosolyma longe clarissima urbium orientis, non Iudaeae modo, et Herodium cum oppido inlustri eiusdem nominis.

Iordanes amnis oritur e fonte Paniade, qui cognomen dedit Caesareae de qua dicemus. Amnis amoenus influit Asphaltiten . . . Asphaltites nihil praeter bitumen gignit, unde et nomen Graecum. Nullum corpus animalium recipit, tauri camelique fluitant; inde fama nihil in eo mergi . . .

Ab occidente litora Esseni fugiunt usque quā nocent, gens sola et in toto orbe praeter ceteras mira, sine ulla femina, omni venere abdicata, sine pecunia, socia palmarum. In diem ex aequo [numero] convenarum turba renascitur large frequentantibus quos vita fessos ad mores eorum fortuna fluctibus agitat. Ita per seculorum milia (incredibile dictu) gens aeterna est in qua nemo nascitur: tam fecunda illis aliorum vitae paenitentia est! 25

Infra hos Engada oppidum fuit, secundum ab Hierosolymis fertilitate palmetorumque nemoribus, nunc alterum bustum. Inde Masada castellum in rupe et ipsum haut procul Asphaltite. Et hactenus Iudaea est. 30

Vocabulary

abdico,-dicare to renounce
Acrebitena,-ae f., modern city of Accrabim
aequus,-a,-um equal
aeternus,-a,-um eternal
agito (1) to drive
alter,altera,alterum another
amnis,-is m., river
amoenus,-a,-um pleasant/delightful
Andromeda,-ae f., Ethiopian king's daughter chained to a rock and exposed to a sea monster but rescued by and married to Perseus
Apollonia,-ae f., a name given to several cities and towns
Arabia,-ae f., Arabia, divided by the ancients into Petraea, Deserta, and Felix
Arabus,-a,-um Arabian
asper,-aspera,asperum rugged
Asphaltites,-is f., the Dead Sea
Bethleptephene,-es f., Bethlebaoth, ancient town south of Judaea in the province of Idumaea, founded by Vespasian
bitumen,bituminis n., asphalt
bustum,-i n., heap of ash/pyre
Caesarea,-ae f., influential commercial and harbor town on the coast of Judaea, built by Herod 22–11 B.C.
camelus,-i m., camel
castellum,-i n., fortress
Coele,-es f., southern part of Syria, known as "Hollow Syria," stretching between Mt. Lebanon and Antilibanis
cognomen,-nominis n., second name
collis,-is m., hill
colonia,-ae f., colony
condo,condere,condidi,conditum to found/establish
confinium,-i n., frontier
consero,-serere,-sevi,-situm to plant
contingo,-tingere,-tigi,-tactum to border
convenae,-arum m. and f. pl., refugees
Damascena,-ae f., the territory of Damascus
deduco,-ducere,-duxi,-ductum to establish
discerno,-cernere,-crevi,-cretum to separate
dispergo,-pergere,-persi,-persum to scatter/cover
distinctus,-a,-um adorned/distinguished
divido,-videre,-visi,-visus to divide
Emmaus,-i m., town established by Vespasian as a military colony
Engada,-ae f., oasis town of Engedi on the southern coast of the Dead Sea, noted for its perfumes and spices
Essenes,-is m., a separatist zealot group that believed in ascetic living and the impending arrival of a messiah
etiamnunc even now
exin adv., then

fecundus,-a,-um prolific/fertile
fertilitas,fertilitatis f., fertility
fessus,-a,-um tired/weary
fluctus,-us m., wave
fluito (1) to float
fons,fontis m., source/spring
frequento (1) to collect in large numbers
fundo,fundere,fudi,fusum to spread
Galilaea,-ae f., the northern province of Palestine in which the Sea of Galilee is located
gigno,gignere,genui,genitum to produce
Gophanitica,-ae f., ancient town of Gophna in the southern province of Idumaea
hactenus adv., as far as this
haut adv., not
Herod,Herodis m., Herod the Great, king of Judaea (40–4 B.C.), who undertook great building works throughout the region
Herodius,-i m., fortress town in the province of Judaea, carved out of a mountaintop by King Herod
Hiericunt,-tis f., oasis town of Jericho in the Jordan River valley near the Dead Sea; one of oldest cities in the world
Hierosolyma,-orum n. pl., town of Jerusalem, important to Jews and Romans as a political and commercial city
Idumaea,-ae f., southern province of Palestine
influo,-fluere,-fluxi,-fluxum to flow into
infra + acc. below
inlustris,-e famous/distinguished
insideo,-sidere to sit on
intus adv., inward
inundatio,-onis f., (the great) flood/inundation
Iope,-is f., Joppa (see below)
Iopica,-ae f., ancient harbor town of Joppa; according to Greek myth, it was named after the mother of Andromeda, saved from the sea monster by Perseus
Iordanes,-is f., the River Jordan, which flows from Panias (Caesarea Philippi) through the Sea of Galilee into the Dead Sea
Iudaea,-ae f., the central province of Judaea in Palestine
iunctus,-a,-um next to/joined
iuxta adv., close by
large adv., largely
longe lateque far and wide
Lydda,-ae f., ancient town seized and destroyed by the proconsul Cestius Gallus on his march to Jersusalem in 65 A.D.
Masada,-ae f., desert fortress in the Negev Desert near the Dead Sea built 37–31 B.C. by Herod the Great.
mergo,mergere,mersi,mersum to sink
mirus,-a,-um remarkable/astonishing
mons,montis m., mountain
namque conj., for
nemus,nemoris n., forest
noceo,nocere to do harm
occidens,-ntis m., the West
occupo (1) to occupy
oppidum,-i n., town/village
orbis,-is m., world
ordo,ordinis m., order/arrangement
oriens,orientis m., the East
Orine,-es f., the Judaean Hills
paenitenia,-ae f., regret/repentance
Palaestine,-es f., Palestine, the land of the Jews, consisting of the provinces of Judaea, Galilee, Idumaea, and Petraea
palma,-ae f., palm tree
palmetum,-i n., palm grove
Panias,-iadis f., ancient town of Panias (Caesarea Philippi), which is the source of the Jordan River
passus,-us m., pace/mile
Peraea,-ae f., eastern province of Palestine
Phoenice,-es f., Phoenicia, the coastal region of Syria
Phoeniceus,-a-um adj., Phoenician
plures,plura several/many
praeiaceo,-iacere to lie in front
praeter except/besides/beyond
Prima Flavia,Primae Flaviae f., name given to Caesarea Palestina by Vespasian
procul adv., far away
proximus,-a,-um nearest/next
quā adv., where
recedo,-cedere,-cessi,-cessum to recede
regio,-onis f., region/country
reliquus,-a,-um remaining
renascor,-nasci,-natus sum to be born again/renew/increase
recipio,-cipere,-cepi,-ceptum to draw in/receive (into a place)
riguus,-a,-um flowing
rupes,-is f., cliff
Samaria,-ae f., ancient town of Samaria, in the province of Judaea, which was renamed Sebaste by King Herod and rebuilt in 27 B.C.
saxum,-i n., rock/detached fragment of rock
seculum,-i n., generation

socia,-ae f., companion
solus,-a,-um solitary
supra + acc. acc. beyond
Syria,-ae f., Syria, the country between Asia Minor and Egypt
taurus,-i m., bull
Thamnitica,-ae f., ancient town of Thamna, near Lydda
toparchia,-ae f., district forming a unit of local government in Judaea and the Hellenistic world
turba,-ae f., throng
turris,-is f., tower; Stratonis turris (tower of Strato) was the earliest name for the site that came to be Caesarea
usque quā to the extent that/as far as
venus,veneris f., sexual desire
vero adv., however/in truth/but
Vespasianus,-i m., Roman emperor 70–79 A.D.
vestigium,-i n., trace/mark
vinculum,-i n., chain/fetter

Man the Highest Species but Dependent on the Others

Grammar Review

Irregular 1st- and 2nd-Declension Adjectives p. 147
Subjunctive Result Clauses pp. 138, 139
Subjunctive Indirect Questions p. 139

New Grammar

Historical infinitives are often used in historical narrative instead of the imperfect indicative to describe actions repeatedly occurring.

> *Cetera animalia* ***sentire*** *naturam suam, alia pernicitatem* ***usurpare****,*
> alia praepetes volatus, alia mare.

> Other animals **sense** their own nature, some **make use of** quickness of
> movement, others swift flight, others the sea.

Alternate accusative and ablative endings for 3rd-declension *i*-stem nouns

	singular	plural
Nom.	serpens = f., serpent	serpentes
Gen.	serpentis	serpentium
Dat.	serpenti	serpentibus
Acc.	serpentem, serpent**im**	serpentes, serpent**is**
Abl.	serpente, serpent**i**	serpentibus

NB:			
	ante omnia		first of all
	cura,-ae		f., anxiety/worry/disquiet
	ne . . . quidem		not even
	Hercule		exclamation, by Hercules!
	in + **abl.**		prep., with
	in + **acc.**		against/toward
	iure		adv., rightly
	per + acc.		prep., for
	serpentis	=	serpentes (acc. pl.)
	sponte **abl.** + gen.		in accordance with

Sentences

1. Principium iure homini tribuetur, cuius causā natura magna videtur genuisse cuncta alia sed tantā saevā mercede ut non sit satis aestimare an natura melior parens homini aut tristior noverca fuerit.
2. Ante omnia unum animantium cunctorum natura opibus alienis velat.
3. Natura tribuit tegimenta cunctis animalibus nisi homini: testas, cortices, spinas, coria, villos, saetas, pilos, plumam, pinnas, squamas, vellera.
4. Hominem tantum nudum natali die in nuda humo abicit statim ad vagitus ploratumque et nullum aliud animalium pronius ad lacrimas est.
5. Prima spes roboris primumque munus temporis eum similem quadripedi facit.
6. Quam diu vertex palpitans est, summum indicium inbecillitatis inter cuncta animalia!
7. Sunt medicinae tantae excogitatae contra mala, sed hae a novis malis subinde vincuntur.
8. Cetera animalium sentiunt naturam suam; nisi doctrinā homo nihil scit, non fari, non ingredi, non vesci et non aliud naturae suae sponte quam flere!
9. Nulli alii vita fragilior est, nulli libido rerum omnium maior, nulli pavor confusior, nulli rabies acrior.
10. Denique cetera animantia in suo genere degunt; ne maris quidem beluae ac pisces nisi in diversa genera saeviunt: at Hercule plurima mala homini ex homine sunt.

Translation

Principium iure tribuetur homini, cuius causa videtur cuncta alia genuisse
natura magna, saeva mercede contra tanta sua munera, ut non sit satis
aestimare, parens melior homini an tristior noverca fuerit. Ante omnia
unum animantium cunctorum alienis velat opibus, ceteris varie tegimenta
tribuit, testas, cortices, spinas, coria, villos, saetas, pilos, plumam, pinnas, 5
squamas, vellera; truncos etiam arboresque cortice, interdum gemino, a
frigoribus et calore tutata est: hominem tantum nudum et in nuda humo
natali die abicit ad vagitus statim et ploratum, nullumque tot animalium
aliud pronius ad lacrimas, et has protinus vitae principio . . .

Prima roboris spes primumque temporis munus quadripedi similem 10
facit. Quando homini incessus! Quando vox! Quando firmum cibis os! Quam
diu palpitans vertex, summae inter cuncta animalia inbecillitatis indicium!
Iam morbi, totque medicinae contra mala excogitatae, et hae quoque subinde
novitatibus victae! Et cetera sentire naturam suam, alia pernicitatem
usurpare, alia praepetes volatus, alia mare: hominem nihil scire nisi 15
doctrina, non fari, non ingredi, non vesci, breviterque non aliud naturae
sponte quam flere! . . . Uni animantium luctus est datus, uni luxuria et
quidem innumeralibus modis ac per singula membra, uni ambitio, uni
avaritia, uni immensa vivendi cupido, uni superstitio, uni sepulturae cura
atque etiam post se de futuro. Nulli vita fragilior, nulli rerum omnium 20
libido maior, nulli pavor confusior, nulli rabies acrior. Denique cetera

animantia in suo genere probe degunt: congregari videmus et stare contra dissimilia—leonum feritas inter se non dimicat, serpentium morsus non petit serpentis, ne maris quidem beluae ac pisces nisi in diversa genera saeviunt: at Hercule homini plurima ex homine sunt mala. 25

Vocabulary

abicio,-icere,-ieci,-iectum to abandon/expose
aestimo (1) to judge
alienus,-a,-um belonging to others
ambitio,-onis f., ambition
animans,-ntis living being
arbor,-oris f., tree
avaritia,-ae f., avarice
belua,-ae f., beast
calor,-oris m., heat
cibus,-i m., food
confusus,-a,-um disturbing/confusing
congrego (1) (usually passive) to assemble/come together in groups
corium,-i n., hide
cortex,-icis m., bark
contra + acc. adv., in return for/against
cunctus,-a,-um all
cupido,-inis f., longing/passionate desire/lust
dego,degere,degi to pass one's time
diversus,-a,-um opposite
devincio,-vincire,-vinxi,-vinctum to fetter
dimico,dimicare,dimicavi to fight/contend
doctrina,-ae f., teaching/instruction
excogito (1) to devise
feritas,-atis f., savageness
firmus,-a,-um strong/stout/durable
fleo,flere,flevi,fletum to weep
for,fari,fatus sum to speak
fragilis,-e fragile
frigus,-oris n., cold/coldness
futurum,-i n., the future
geminus,-a,-um double
gigno,gignere,genui,genitum to produce
humus,-i f., earth/dry ground
immensus,-a,-um vast/immense
inbecillitas,-atis f., physical weakness
incessus,-us m., walking/walk
indicium,-i n., mark/sign
ingredior,-gredi,-gressus sum to walk
innumeralis,-e adj., innumerable
interdum adv., sometimes
lacrima,-ae f., tear
leo,leonis m., a lion
libido,-inis f., desire/wish/fancy
luctus,-us m., expression of grief
luxuria,-ae f., indulgence/extravagance
medicina,-ae f., remedy/treatment/cure
membrum,-i n., limb/member of the body
merces,-edis f., price
morbus,-i m., disease/illness
morsus,-us m., a bite
munus,-eris n., gift
natalis,-is m., day of one's birth
noverca,-ae f., stepmother
novitas,-atis f., new
nudus,-a,-um naked/nude
ops,opis f., resource/natural gift
os,oris n., mouth
palpito (1) to beat/pulsate
parens,-ntis m., parent
pavor,-oris m., sudden fear/terror/fright
pernicitas,-atis f., quickness of movement
pilus,-i m., a hair
pinna,-ae f., feather
piscis,-is m., fish
ploratus,-us m., crying
pluma,-ae f., down of an animal
praepes,-etis adj., swift
principium,-i n., first place
probe adv., rightly/properly
pronus,-a,-um inclined to/prone
protinus adv., immediately
quadrupes,-edis adj., four-footed animal
quando interrog. adv., when?
rabies,-ei f., savageness/ferocity
robur,roboris n., physical strength
saeta,-ae f., bristles

saevio,saevire,saevii,saevitum to act ferociously/rage/be violent
saevus,-a,-um savage
sentio,sentire,sensi,sensum to sense
sepultura,-ae f., burial/place of burial
serpens,-ntis f., serpent
singulus,-a,-um individual/singular
spina,-ae f., spine
sponte abl. + gen. in accordance with
squama,-ae f., scale of fish
statim adv., immediately
subinde adv., immediately/shortly afterward
superstitio,-onis f., superstition
supplicium,-i n., entreaty
tantum adv., only
tegimentum,-i n., covering/protection
testa,-ae f., shell
tribuo,tribuere,tribui,tributum to ascribe/allot/assign
tristis,-e harsh
truncus,-i m., trunk (of a tree)
tutor,tutari,tutatus sum to protect
usurpo,usurpare to make use of/appropriate
vagitus,-us m., wailing
varie adv., variously/in different ways
vellus,-eris n., fleece
vertex,-icis m., top most part of head
vescor,vesci to eat
villus,-i m., shaggy hair
velo (1) to cover/clothe
volatus,-us m., flight
vox,vocis f., voice

Who Is the Happiest of Mankind?
Vain Mortality Is Ingenious to Compute Happiness in the Manner of a Thracian Clan

Grammar Review

Gerundive of Purpose
Partitive Genitive
Passive Periphrastic

New Grammar

The accusative case is frequently used in exclamatory statements:

Quam multos! How many (men)!

Alius . . . *de alio* (one . . . one way . . . another . . . another way) is an idiom.

Alius de alio *iudicat dies.*

One day judges **one way another** day, **another way**.

The indefinite pronouns ***si quis/si quid*** and the negative forms ***ne quis/ne quid*** follow the same declension pattern as that of the interrogative pronouns.

Nom.	***si quis***	if anyone	***si quid***	if anything
Gen.	***si cuius***	if of anyone	***si cuius***	if anything
Dat.	***si cui***	if to anyone	***si cui***	if anything
Acc.	***si quem***	etc	***si quid***	etc.
Abl.	***si quo***	etc.	***si quo***	etc.

Nom.	***ne quis***	not anyone	***ne quid***	not anything
Gen.	***ne cuius***	not of anyone	***ne cuius***	not of anything
Dat.	***ne cui***	not to anyone	***ne cui***	not to anything
Acc.	***ne quem***	etc	***ne quid***	etc
Abl.	***ne quo***	etc.	***ne quo***	etc.

NB:			
	*adflix**ere***	=	*adflix**erunt***
	bona,-orum		n. pl., property/wealth/good things
	pro + abl.		prep. according to
	quisque/quidque		each
	quid quod?		what that? (i.e., what about the fact that?)

Sentences

1. Mortalitas est vana et ingeniosa; conputat laetitiam ad circumscribendam se.
2. Thracia gens calculos colore distinctos in urnam condit.
3. Gens calculos dinumerat ac iudicium pronunciat.
4. Alius de alio iudicat dies et tantum supremus dies de omnibus diebus.
5. Bona non sunt paria numero malis nec ulla laeititia minimo maerore pensatur.

Translation

. . .Vana mortalitas et ad circumscribendam se ipsam ingeniosa conputat more Thraciae gentis, quae calculos colore distinctos pro experimento cuiusque diei in urnam condit ac supremo die separatos dinumerat atque ita de quoque pronunciat. Quid quod ipse calculi candore illo laudatus dies originem mali habuit? Quam multos accepta adflixere imperia! Quam 5
multos bona perdidere et ultimis mersere suppliciis! Ista nimirum bona, si cui inter illa hora in gaudio fuit! Ita est profecto, alius de alio iudicat dies et tantum supremus de omnibus, ideoque nullis credendum est. Quid quod bona malis paria non sunt etiam pari numero, nec laetitia ulla minimo maerore pensanda? Heu vana et imprudens diligentia! Numerus dierum 10
conputatur, ubi quaeritur pondus!

Vocabulary

adfligo,-fligere,-flixi,-flictum to knock down/overthrow/ruin
bona,-orum n. pl., property/wealth/good things
calculus,-i m., stone
candor,-oris m., whiteness/brilliance
circumscribo,-scribere,-scripsi,-scriptum to deceive
color, coloris m., color
condo,condere,condidi,conditum to store/put away
conputo (1) to calculate
diligentia,-ae f., carefulness/attentiveness
dinumero (1) to count out
distinctus,-a,-um different/distinct
experimentum,-i n., experience
gaudium,-i n., gladness/delight
heu interj., alas!/oh!
ideo adv., for that reason
imprudens,-entis ignorant/imprudent
ingeniosus,-a,-um ingenious/clever
iudico (1) to judge
laetitia,-ae f., joy/happiness
maeror,-oris m., grief/mourning
mergo,mergere,mersi,mersum to plunge/sink/overwhelm
minimus,-a,-um smallest/tiniest
mortalitas,-atis f., mortality
nimirum adv., undoubtedly/certainly
origo,-inis f., source
penso (1) to counterbalance/pay for
perdo,perdere,perdidi,perditum to cause ruin to/destroy
pondus,-oris n., weight/consequence
pro + abl. prep. according to
profecto adv., indeed
pronuncio (1) to publicly declare a decision/judge
quaero,quaerere,quaesivi,quaesitum to seek/ask
quid quod? what that? (i.e., what about the fact that?)

quisque,quidque each one/each thing
separatus,-a,-um separate
supplicium,-i n., punishment/torment
supremus,-a,-um last
tantum adv., only
Thracius,-a,-um Thracian
ultimus,-a,-um most extreme/gravest
urna,-ae f., urn
vanus,-a,-um delusive/untrustworthy

Cases of and Roman Respect of Intellectual Eminence

VI

Grammar Review

Ablative Absolutes	p. 150
Infinitives of Indirect Statement	p. 131
Subjunctive Jussive Noun Clauses	p. 139
Locative Case	
Passive Periphrastic	
Special Ablatives as the Idea of the Whole	

New Grammar

Impersonal verbs appear in 3rd-person singular; the subject is translated as "*it*." Common impersonal verbs include:

accidit **it** happens	*evenit* **it** turns out
constat **it** is well known	*licet* **it** is permitted/allowed
convenit **it** is agreed	*taedet* **it** bores

Ablatives of comparison occur with comparatives and are translated as *than*:

Homero vate Graeco *nullum felicius extitisse convenit.*

It is agreed that no one has stood out more successfully **than the Greek poet Homer**.

Shortened Perfect Active Stems

In verbs with a perfect active stem ending in *–avi* , the ***–vi*** is often left out in the perfect active infinitive and the pluperfect active subjunctive.

*significa**sse*** = *significa**visse***   *significa**sse**t* = *significa**visse**t*

Alternate pluperfect indicative and perfect infinitive forms

usus ***fuerat*** *= usus* ***erat*** *miraturus* ***fuisse*** *= miraturus* ***esse***

The deliberative subjunctive is used in questions and exclamations implying doubt or the impossibility of an action.

Quis ***possit*** *agere delectum gloriae ingeniorum?*

Who **would be able** to make a choice of the renown of geniuses?

Declension pattern of 3rd-declension Greek proper nouns ending in *–es,-is*:

Nom.	Thucydides
Gen.	Thucydidis
Dat.	Thucydidi
Acc.	Thucydiden
Abl.	Thucydide

NB:			
	alias		adv., otherwise
	egere	=	eg*erunt*
	felix,felicis		successful
	Hercule		exclam., by Hercules
	idem,eadem,idem		(in the sense of) likewise
	itaque		adv., for that reason
	obviam+ dat.		adv., to meet
	optumus	=	*optimus*
	quam maxime		as much as possible
	sive . . . sive		whether . . . or . . .
	tam		adv., so far

Legatio trium sapientiae ab Athenis (Legation of three men of wisdom from Athens)

In 157 B.C. the Athenians carried out a raid (possibly for legal claims) against the border town of Oropus and sacked the city. In 156 B.C. Oropus in a suit for reparations appealed to Rome since the Achaean League, a confederation of Greek states, had allied itself with Rome. The Roman Senate appointed the Sicyonians to arbitrate between Oropus and Athens. The Sicyonians assessed a fine on Athens of 500 talents. In 155 B.C. a delegation of three men (Carneades the Academic, Diogenas the Stoic, and Critolaus the Peripatetic), representing the three schools of philosophy in Athens, was sent to Rome by the Athenians to appeal the fine.

Synopsis of Translation

Homer—The highest example of eminent men of literature
Alexander the Great—
How he honored the works of Homer

How he honored the home and family of Pindar at Thebes
How he honored the home of Aristotle
Apollo of Delphi
How he avenged the murder of the poet Archilochus
Father Liber (Bacchus)
How he honored Sophocles the Athenian tragedian
Admonition to Lysander, the Spartan king
Lysander obeys
Dionysius the tyrant of Syracuse
How he honored Plato the master of philosophy
Aeschines the orator
How he honored at a lecture in Rhodes his opponent, the orator Demosthenes
Isocrates the Greek rhetorician
The selling price for one of his speeches
The Athenians
How they honored their exiled general Thucydides
Roman recognition of intellectual eminence
Pompey for the philosopher Posidonius
Cato's fear of the philosopher Carneades
The Elder (Scipio) Africanus for the Roman poet Ennius
The Emperor Augustus for the poet Vergil

Sentences

1. Quis possit agere delectum gloriae ingeniorum?
2. Convenit nullum extitisse felicius Homero vate Graeco.
3. Inter spolia Darii regis Persarum, Alexander scrinium unguentorum cepit. Amicis demonstrantibus usus varios eius scrinii, Alexander inquit: "Detur custodiae librorum Homeri."
4. Etiam Alexander parcebat familiae penatibusquc poetae Pindari, cum Thebas raperet. Et Alexander credidit patriam Aristotelis philosophi esse suam patriam.
5. Liber pater iussit Lysandrum regem Lacedaemonium sepelire defunctum Sophoclem.
6. Dionysius tyrannus ad Platonem philosophum navem vittatam misit.
7. Aeschines Rhodiis defensionem Demosthenis legit.
8. Athenienses Thucydiden imperatorem in exilium egere, Thucydiden conditorem revocavere.
9. Pompeius Magnus intraturus domum Posidonii sapientiae clari forem percuti a lictore vetuit, et fasces litterarum ianuae summisit.

10. Cum Cato censor Carneadem philosophum dicentem audivisset, censuit eum dimittendum esse.
11. Prior Africanus iussit statuam Q. Ennii inponi suo sepulchro.
12. Divus Augustus carmina Vergilii cremari contra testamentum eius vetuit.

Chapter VI

Translation

Ingeniorum gloriae quis possit agere delectum per tot disciplinarum genera
et tantam rerum operumque varietatem? Nisi forte Homero vate Graeco
nullum felicius extitisse convenit, sive operis forma sive materie aestimetur.
Itaque Alexander Magnus inter spolia Darii Persarum regis unguentorum
scrinio capto quod erat de auro margaritis gemmisque pretiosum, varios 5
eius usus amicis demonstrantibus, quando taedebat unguenti bellatorem et
militia sordidum, 'Immo Hercule,' inquit, 'librorum Homeri custodiae
detur,' ut pretiosissimum humani animi opus quam maxime diviti opere
servaretur. Idem Pindari vatis familiae penatibusque iussit parci cum
Thebas raperet, Aristotelis philosophi patriam suam credidit, tantaeque 10
rerum claritati tam benignum testimonium miscuit. Archilochi poetae
interfectores Apollo arguit Delphis. Sophoclem tragici cothurni principem
defunctum sepelire Liber pater iussit, obsidentibus moenia Lacedaemoniis,
Lysandro eorum rege in quiete saepius admonito ut pateretur humari
delicias suas. Requisivit rex, qui supremum diem Athenis obissent nec 15
difficulter ex his quem deus significasset intellexit, pacemque funeri dedit.

Platoni sapientiae antistiti Dionysius tyrannus alias saevitiae
superbiaeque natus vittatam navem misit obviam, ipse quadrigis albis
egredientem in litore excepit. Viginti talentis unam orationem Isocrates
vendidit. Aeschines Atheniensis summus orator, cum accusationem qua fuerat 20
usus Rhodiis legisset, legit et defensionem Demosthenis qua in illud depulsus

fuerat exilium, mirantibusque tum magis fuisse miraturos dixit si ipsum orantem audivissent, calamitate testis ingens factus inimici. Thucydiden imperatorem Athenienses in exilium egere, rerum conditorem revocavere, eloquentiam mirati cuius virtutem damnaverant. 25

Perhibuere et Romani proceres etiam exteris testimonia. Cn. Pompeius confecto Mithridatico bello intraturus Posidonii sapientiae professione clari domum forem percuti de more a lictore vetuit, et fasces litterarum ianuae summisit is cui se oriens occidensque summiserat. Cato censorius in illa nobili trium sapientiae procerum ab Athenis legatione 30 audito Carneade quamprimum legatos eos censuit dimittendos, quoniam illo viro argumentante quid veri esset haut facile discerni posset.

Sed et nostrorum gloriam percenseamus. Prior Africanus Q. Ennii statuam sepulchro suo inponi iussit, clarumque illud nomen, immo vero spolium ex tertia orbis parte raptum, in cinere supremo cum poetae titulo 35 legi. Divus Augustus carmina Vergilii cremari contra testamenti eius verecundiam vetuit, maiusque ita vati testimonium contigit quam si ipse sua probavisset.

Vocabulary

accusatio,-onis f., indictment (of Demosthenes the orator)
admoneo,-monere,-monui,-monitum to admonish
Aeschines,-is m., Athenian orator; bitter enemy of Demosthenes; ultimately goes into voluntary exile in Rhodes
aestimo (1) to rate/judge
Africanus,-i m., Africanus, the elder Scipio
albus,-a,-um white
Alexander,-dri m., Alexander the Great, king of Macedonia
alias adv., otherwise
antistes,-stitis m., master (of any art)
Apollo,-inis m., god of music, poetry, and the sun
Archilochus,-i m., Greek satirical poet
Aristoteles,-is m., Aristotle, the Greek philosopher

argumentor,argumentari to argue/allege something as fact
arguo,arguere,argui,argutum to expose/reveal
Athenae,-arum f. pl., Athens
Atheniensis,-e Athenian
Augustus,-i m., name granted to Octavius as emperor
aurum,-i n., gold
bellator,-oris m., warrior
benignus,-a,-um kind/generous
calamitas,-atis f., disaster
carmen,-inis n., poem/poetry
Carneades,-is m., 214–129 B.C., a skeptic philosopher of Cyrene. By 159 B.C. he had become head of the Academy (the school of philosophy founded by Plato) in Athens. He was one of three philosophers sent to Rome in 155 B.C. by the Athenians to appeal a fine that had been assessed on them by Rome. His lectures on the uncertainty of justice caused consternation among the leading politicians.
Cato,-onis m., 234–149 B.C., Marcus Cato the Elder, commonly surnamed Censorius (the Censor)
censeo,censere,censui,censum to vote/recommend
censorius,-i m., one who has held the office of censor/the censor
cinis,-eris m., ash
claritas,-atis f., renown
conditor,-oris m., author
conficio,-ficere,-feci,-fectum to conclude
contingo,-tingere,-tigi,-tactum + dat. to befall/happen
contra adv., against
convenit impers, it is agreed
cothurnus,-i tragicus,-i m., Greek tragedian
cremo (1) to burn
custodia,-ae f., guardianship/care
Cypria,-ae f., Cyprus
damno (1) to condemn
Darius,-i m., king of Persia
defensio,-onis f., defense
defungor,-fungi,-functus sum to die
delectus,-us m., choosing/choice
deliciae,-arum f. pl., beloved objects/favorites
Delphi,-orum m. pl., Delphi, home of the oracle of Apollo
demonstro (1) to point out
Demosthenes,-is m., 4th-century B.C. Athenian orator
depello,-pellere,-pulsi,-pulsum to drive away
difficulter adv., with difficulty
dimitto,-mittere,-misi,-missum to send away
Dionysius,-i m., tyrant ruler of Syracuse
discerno,-cernere,-crevi,-cretum to discern/separate
disciplina,-ae f., instruction/teaching
dives,divitis costly/rich
divus,-a,-um deified
egredior,egredi,egressus sum to step out/disembark
eloquentia,-ae f., eloquence
etenim conj., for indeed
excipio,-cipere,-cepi,-ceptum to receive
exilium,-i n., exile
exto,-tare,-titi to stand out
exterus,-a,-um foreign
familia,-ae f., household/family
fasces,-ium m. pl., symbols of Roman authority (bundles of sticks along with an axe carried by lictors before chief Roman magistrates)
felix,-icis successful
foris,-is f., door
forte adv., perhaps
funus,-eris n., burial/funeral
gemma,-ae f., precious stone
haud/haut adv., not at all/by no means
Homerus,-i m., Homer, the Greek epic poet
humo (1) to bury
ianua,-ae f., door/portal
immo on the contrary
imperator,-oris m., general/military commander
ingens,ingentis enormous
ingeniousus,-a,-um talented
ingenium,-i n., genius
inimicus,-i m., enemy
inpono,-ponere,-posui,-positum to place
interfector,-oris m., murderer
invidia,-ae f., envy/jealousy
intro (1) to enter
Isocrates,-is m., famous Athenian rhetorician and educator
Lacedaemon,-onis f., Spartan
legatio,-onis f., legation/embassy
legatus,-i m., legate/envoy
Liber,-eri m., Bacchus, god of wine
lictor,-oris m., public attendants who executed the sentences of the Roman magistrates
lingua,-ae f., language
Lysander,-dri m., famous Spartan general
Marcus,-i Varro,-onis 116–27 B.C., soldier and polymath, by universal consent the most learned Roman of his day

Macedonia,-ae f., Macedonia
margarita,-ae f., pearl
materies,materiei f., literary content
memorabilis,-e remarkable
milis,-itis m., soldier
militia,-ae f., warfare
miror,mirari,miratus sum to admire/revere
misceo,miscere,miscui,mixtum to unite/blend
Mithridates,-is m., Mithridates VI, king of Pontus
Mithridaticus,-a,-um relating to Mithridates
moenia,-ium n. pl., walls/fortifications of a city
natus,-a,-um (fitted) by nature
navalis,-e naval
nobilis,-e renowned/celebrated
obeo,-ire,-ii,-itum + supremum diem to die
obsideo,-sidere,-sedi,-sessum to besiege
occidens,-dentis west
oratio,-onis f., speech
oriens,-ntis east
parco,parcere,peperci + dat. to spare/show consideration for
patior,pati,passus sum to permit
penates,-ium m., pl.dwelling\house
percenseo,-censere,-censui to review
percutio,-cutere,-cussi,-cussum to knock/strike
perhibeo,-hibere,-hibui,-hibitum to bring forward/cite
Persarae,-arum f., Persian
philosophus,-i m., philosopher
Pindarus,-i m., lyric poet of Thebes
Plato,-onis m., Plato, celebrated Greek philosopher
Posidonius,-i m., Stoic philospher
pretiosus,-a,-um of great value/precious
princeps,-cipis adj., foremost/first
prior,-oris elder
probo (1) to find good/approve
procer,-eris m., noble
professio,-onis f., profession/art
pronepos,-potis m., great grandson
quadrigae,-arum f., a team of four horses (drawing a chariot)
quamprimum adv., as soon as possible
quando adv., since
quies,-etis f., rest
Quintus,-i Ennius,-i m., father of Roman poetry
rapio,rapere,rapui,raptum to plunder/sack
reliquus,-a,-um left behind
Rhodius,-a,-um f., Rhodian/of Rhodes, an island near the coast of Asia Minor
requiro,-quiere,-quisivi,-quisitum to ask
revoco (1) to recall
saevitia,-ae f., rage/ferocity
scrinium,-i n., case/box
sepelio,-pelire,-pelivi,-pultum to bury/be buried
sepulcrum,-i n., tomb
servo (1) to keep
significo (1) to indicate
Sophocles,-is m., the Greek tragic poet
sordidus,-a,-um dirty
spolium,-i n., spoils/booty
statua,-ae f., statue
summitto,-mittere,-misi,-misum to submit/yield; **summittere fasces** to lower the fasces as a sign of respect
superbus,-a,-um exalted/haughty
superbia,-ae f., arrogance
taedet,taedere,taeduit,taesum est 3rd impers. (with acc. of thing affected and gen. of thing toward which feeling is directed); it wearies/bores
talentum,-i n., Greek monetary weight; approx. half a hundred weight of coins
testamentum,-i n., last will
testimonium,-i n., witness/testimony
testis,-is m., witness
Thebae,-arum f., Thebes
Thucydides,-is m., the Athenian general and historian
titulus,-i m., commemorative inscription
tres,tria three
unguentum,-i n., perfume
universus,-a,-um all
usus,-us m., use
Uticensis,-e of Utica, a town in Africa north of Carthage
varietas,-atis f., variety/diversity
varius,-a,-um various
vates,-is m., poet
vendo,vendere,vendidi,venditum to sell
verecundia,-ae f., modesty
Vergilius,-i m., Vergil, the famous Roman poet
vero in truth/really
veto,vetare,vetui,vetitum to forbid
vittatus,-a,-um bound with garlands

Exceptional Examples of Multiple Births

Grammar Review

Special Ablatives as the Idea of the Whole
Irregular Comparative Adjectives p. 148
Locative Case

New Grammar

Duration of time is occasionally expressed by the ablative case.

> ***supremis*** *divi Augusti* = **during the funeral rites** of the divine Augustus

Distributive numerals are plural adjectives that tell how many of each or how many at a time.

bini,-ae,-a	two at at time/two by two
quini,-ae,-a	five at a time/five times
septeni,-ae,-a	seven at a time/seven times

Translation

Tergeminos nasci certum est Horatiorum Curiatiorumque exemplo; super inter ostenta ducitur praeterquam in Aegypto, ubi fetifer potu Nilus amnis. Proxime supremis divi Augusti Fausta quaedam e plebe Ostiae duos mares totidemque feminas enixa famem quae consecuta est portendit haud dubie. Reperitur et in Peloponneso quinos quater enixa, maioremque partem ex (5) omni eius vixisse partu. Et in Aegypto septenos uno utero simul gigni auctor est Trogus.

Vocabulary

Aegyptus,-i f., Egypt
amnis,-is m., river
Fausta,-ae f., proper noun
consequor,-sequi,-secutus sum to follow
Curati,-orum m. pl., ancient and famous Roman family
divus,-a,-um m., divine
enitor,eniti,enixus sum to bring forth/bear
exemplum,-i n., example
fames,famis f., famine
Fausta,-ae f., Fausta
fetifer,fetifera,fetiferum causing fruitfulness
gigno,gignere,genui,genitum to bring forth/to bear
haud dubie adv., undoubtedly
Horatii,-orum m. pl., ancient and famous Roman family
mas,maris m., male
nascor,nasci,natus sum to be born
Nilus,-i m., Nile River
ostentum,-i n., prodigy/portent
Ostia,-ae f., port city of Rome
partus,-us m., a birth
plebs,plebis f., the common people
portendo,-tendere,-tendi,-tentum to indicate/predict
potus,-us m., a drinking/draught
Peloponnesus,-i m., southern part of Greece
praeterquam adv., except
proxime adv., recently
quater adv., four times
quini,-ae,-a five at a time (i.e., quintuplets)
septeni,-ae,-a seven times
simul adv., at the same time
super adv., above (this number)
suprema,-orum n. pl., funeral rites
tergemini,-orum m. pl., triplets
totidem adv., just as many
Trogus,-i Pompeius,-i m., Roman historian flourishing at the time of Augustus; writer of the treatise *De Animalibus*
uterus,-us m., womb
vinco,vincere,vixi,victum to survive

Invention of Writing and First Agreements Between Nations

New Grammar

Early 2nd-declension noun nominative singular ending was ***-os*** instead of *–us*. ***divos,-i*** = m., god

Nom.	***divos*** *(divus)*
Gen.	*divi*
Dat.	*divo*
Acc.	*divum*
Abl.	*divo*

Roman historical timekeeping is dated from the founding of the city: 753 AUC (*ab urbe condita*) is the traditionally accepted foundation date.

Pliny often uses the ablative case to denote duration of time:

Nec congruebant ad horas eius liniae, paruerunt tamen ei ***annis undecentum****.*

Nor the lines corresponded to its hours, nevertheless they followed this **for 99 years**.

Verbs of agreeing, resolving, deciding, permitting are followed by Subjunctive Noun Clauses.

Conspiravit ***ut litteris Ionum uterentur****.*

It was agreed **that they use (benefit themselves by means of) the Ionian alphabet.**

NB:			
	ad + acc.		near
	ante . . . quam		before
	apud		in the writings of
	Cos.		consul
	fuere	=	*fuerunt*
	in + abl.		concerning
	post . . . quam		after
	ratio,rationis		theory/science
	secundum + acc		alongside
	ut auctor est Varro		Varro relates
	venere	=	venerunt

Sentences

1. Primus consensus omnium gentium conspiravit ut litteris Ionum uterentur.
2. Sequens gentium consensus fuit in tonsoribus, sed Romanis tonsores serius venerunt.
3. Tertius consensus fuit in horarum observatione, quae ratio reperiebatur in Graecia.
4. In XII tabulis, tantum ortus et occasus nominantur, et post aliquot annos, meridies adiectus est, accenso consulum id pronuntiante a curia cum prospexisset solem inter Rostra et Graecostasim.
5. Fabius Vestalis prodit Lucium Papirium Cursorem statuisse primum solarium horologium undecim annos ante bellum cum Pyrro, sed Fabius non significat rationem horologi vel artificem nec dicit unde translatum sit.

Translation

Gentium consensus tacitus primus omnium conspiravit ut Ionum litteris uterentur . . .

Sequens gentium consensus in tonsoribus fuit, sed Romanis tardior. In Italiam ex Sicilia venere post Romam conditam anno CCCCLIV adducente P. Titinio Mena, ut auctor est Varro; antea intonsi fuere. Primus omnium radi cotidie instituit Africanus sequens. Divos Augustus cultris semper usus est.

Tertius consensus fuit in horarum observatione, iam hic ratione accedens, quando et a quo in Graecia reperta, diximus secundo volumine. Serius etiam hoc Romae contigit: XII tabulis ortus tantum et occasus nominantur, post aliquot annos adiectus est et meridies, accenso consulum id pronuntiante cum a curia inter Rostra et Graecostasim prospexisset solem. A columna Maenia ad carcerem inclinato sidere supremam (horam) pronuntiavit, sed hoc serenis tantum diebus, usque ad primum Punicum bellum. Princeps Romanis solarium horologium statuisse ante undecim annos quam cum Pyrro bellatum est ad aedem Quirini.

L. Papirius Cursor, cum eam dedicaret a patre suo votam, a Fabio Vestale proditur; sed neque facti horologi rationem vel artificem significat nec unde translatum sit aut apud quem scriptum id invenerit. M. Varro primum [horologium] statutum in publico secundum Rostra in columna tradit bello Punico primo a M. Valerio Messala cos. Catina capta in Sicilia.

. . . Nec congruebant ad horas eius liniae, paruerunt tamen ei annis undecentum, donec Q. Marcius Philippus qui cum L. Paullo fuit censor diligentius ordinatum (horologium) iuxta posuit. Etiam tum tamen nubilo incertae fuere horae usque ad proximum lustrum; tunc Scipio Nasica 25 collega Laenatis primus aqua divisit horas aeque noctium ac dierum, idque horologium sub tecto dicavit anno urbis DXCV: tamdiu populo Romano indiscreta lux fuit.

Vocabulary

accedo,-cedere,-cessi,-cessum to approach/be added
accensus,-i m., attendant
adduco,-ducere,-duxi,-ductum to import/bring from abroad
adicio,-icere,-ieci,-iectum to add
aedes,aedis f., temple
aeque adv., equally
aes,aeris n., bronze
Africanus sequens (the second Africanus) Scipio Aemilianus, consul 147 and 134 B.C.; adopted son of Scipio Africanus, consul 205 and 194; conqueror of Spain, Africa, and Asia Minor
aliquot adv., several
antea adv., before then
ante . . . quam before
aqua,-ae f., water
artifex,artificis m., craftsman/artist
Augustus,-i m., the Emperor Augustus
bello (1) to wage war
carcer,carceris m., prison
Catina,-ae f., modern-day Catania, a town on the east coast of Sicily
censor,censoris m., censor
collega,-ae m., colleague/associate
columna,-ae f., column
columna Maenia f., pillar in the Roman Forum to which thieves and slaves were tied to receive punishment
condo,condere,condidi,conditum to build
congruo,congruere,congrui to correspond/agree with
consensus,-us m., agreement
conspiro (1) to agree
consul,consulis m., consul
contingo,-tingere,-tigi,-tactum to happen
cotidie adv., daily
culter,cultri m., razor
curia,-ae f., Senate house
dedico (1) to dedicate
Delphicus,-a,-um of Delphi
dico (1) to dedicate
diligenter adv., carefully
divido,dividere,divisi,divisum to divide/distribute
divos,-i m., god
donec conj., while/as long as/until
Fabius,-i Vestalis,-is m., a Latin author cited by Pliny
Graecostasis,-is f., the building in the Roman Forum for lodging Greeks and other foreign ambassadors
gratus,-a,-um grateful/pleasing
hodie adv., today/still/even now
horologium,-i n., a sundial
inclinatus,-a,-um sinking/inclined
indiscretus,-a,-um undivided
instituo,instituere,institui, institutum to resolve/begin
intonsus,-a,-um unshaven/with a beard
Iones,Ionum m. pl., Ionians, Greek-speaking people of Asia Minor
iuxta adv., nearby
L. Papirius,-i Cursor,-oris m., a Roman consul of 3rd-century B.C.

L. Paullus,-i m., Roman censor, 164 B.C.
linia,-ae f., line
lustrum,-i n., a sacrifice for expiation and purification offered by one of the Roman censors at the close of the taking of the census every five years
lux,lucis f., daylight
Marcus,-i Popillius,-i Laenas,-atis m., Roman censor, 159 B.C.
Marcus-i Varro,-onis m., author and praetor; 116 B.C.–27 B.C.
Marcus,-i Valerius,-i Messala,-ae m., a Roman consul of late 1st century B.C.
meridies,meridiei m., midday/noon
nomino (1) to mention/name
nubilum,-i n., cloudy weather
observatio,observationis f., observation
occasus,-us m., sunset
ordinatus,-a,-um calibrated
ortus,-us m., sunrise
P. Titinius,-i Mena,-ae m., Roman general who brought barbers from Sicily to Rome
paene adv., nearly/almost
Palatium,-i n., Palatine Hill
pareo,parere,parui + dat. to obey/follow/be obedient to
pono,ponere,posui,positum to set up/erect
post . . . quam after
princeps,principis adj., first
prodo,prodere,prodidi,proditum to relate/hand down
pronuntio (1) to proclaim/announce
prospicio,-spicere,-spexi,-spectum to make out in the distance/see/observe
proximus,-a,-um next
publicus,-a,-um public
Punicum,-i bellum,-i war between Rome and Carthage; First Punic War 264–241; Second Punic War 218–201; Third Punic War 149–146
Pyrrus,-i m., Pyrrhus of Epirus, led a mercenary army into Italy in 280 B.C.
Q. Marcius Philippus m., Roman censor 164 B.C.
Quirinus,-i m., Quirinus was most likely a Sabine god. The Sabines had a settlement near the eventual site of Rome and erected an altar to Quirinus on the Collis Quirinalis, or Quirinal Hill, one of the Seven Hills of Rome. When the Romans settled there, they absorbed the cult of Quirinus into their early belief system; he was said to be the deified Romulus.
rado,radere,rasi,rasum to shave
ratio,rationis f., theory/science
Rostra,Rostrorum n. pl., speaker's platform in the Forum
Scipio,-onis Nasica,-ae m., Publius Cornelius Scipio Nasica, consul in 191; chosen in 204 as the noblest and morally best of the Romans
secundum + acc. alongside
sequens,-ntis second/next
serenus,-a,-um clear
serius adv., rather late
Sicilia,-ae f., Sicily
sidus,sideris n., sun (in this reading)
significo (1) to show/list
solarium,-i n., sundial/clock
statuo,statere,statui,statutum to build/erect
supremus,-a,-um last
tabulae,-arum f. pl., the Twelve Tables, the first Roman Law Code, set up in the Forum as permanent record
tacitus,-a,-um silent/secret
tamdiu adv., for so long a time
tantum adv., only
tardus,-a,-um late
tectum,-i n., cover/shelter/roof
tonsor,tonsoris m., barber
transfero,-ferre,-tuli,-latum to transfer/copy
unde adv., from where
undecentum indeclin. adj., ninety-nine
usque adv., until
vel conj., or
volumen,voluminis n., book
voveo,vovere,vovi,votum to vow

Lions: Their Taming, Their Mercifulness and Gratitude

Grammar Review

Subjunctive Cum Clauses	p. 139
Jussive Subjunctive	p. 138
Gerunds	p. 131
eo,ire,ii,itum	p. 132

New Grammar

Ablatives of degree of difference occur with comparatives.

> ***multo*** *diutius* = for a **much** longer time (literally, a longer time by much)

Ablatives of cause denote cause and are translated *on account of/because of*

> *Multoque diutius* ***miraculo*** *quam* ***metu*** *cessatur.*
>
> And for a much longer time there is hesitation/action is delayed **on account of amazement** more than **because of fear** (of what might happen).

NB:			
	ad + acc.		near/nearby
	autem		adversative conj., but/on the other hand
	iere	=	*ierunt*
	in tantum		as well as
	neque . . . et		not only . . . but
	opus est/esset		to be needed/necessary/required
	qua maxime		in which ever way best
	sese	=	*se*
	set (sed)		and indeed
	tam		adv., to such a degree/so much

Sentences

1. Marcus Antonius primus iugo leones subdidit et ad currum eos iunxit cum in campis Pharsaliis civile bellum dimicaretur.

2. Hanno, Poenus erat primus qui manu leonem tractavit ut ostenderet leonem mansuefactum.

3. Syracusanus Mentor, cum in Syria leonem volutantem suppliciterque lambentem sua vestigia conspiceret, animadvertit vulnus tumoremque in pede leonis. Extracto surculo leonem cruciatu liberavit: pictura casum hunc testatur Syracusis.

4. Elpis Samius delatus ad Africam nave conspexit leonem iuxta litus hiatu minaci et Elpis arborem fuga petivit. Os morsu avidiore inhaeserat dentibus leonis. Non solum inedia cruciabat leonem sed etiam poena de telis eius ipsis.

5. Dum fortuita fides non est contra feram suspectantem et velut mutis precibus orantem, multoque diutius miraculo quam metu cessatur. Set degressus arborem, evellit os leoni praebenti adcommmodantique hiatum qua maxime opus esset. Leo retulit suam gratiam venatus suos adgerendo ad Elpem.

Translation

. . . Iugo subdidit (leones) eos primusque Romae ad currum iunxit M. Antonius, et quidem civili bello cum dimicatum esset in Pharsaliis campis, non sine ostento quodam temporum, generosos spiritus iugum subire illo prodigio significante. Nam quod ita vectus est cum mima Cytheride, super monstra etiam illarum calamitatum fuit. Primus autem hominum leonem manu tractare ausus et ostendere mansuefactum Hanno e clarissimis Poenorum traditur damnatusque illo argumento, quoniam nihil non persuasurus vir tam artificis ingenii videbatur, et male credi libertas ei cui in tantum cessisset etiam feritas.

Sunt vero et fortuitae eorum quoque clementiae exempla. Mentor Syracusanus in Syria leone obvio suppliciter volutante attonitus pavore, cum refugienti undique fera opponeret sese et vestigia lamberet adulanti similis, animadvertit in pede eius tumorem vulnusque; extracto surculo liberavit cruciatu: pictura casum hunc testatur Syracusis. Simili modo Elpis Samius natione in Africam delatus nave iuxta litus conspecto leone hiatu minaci arborem fuga petit Libero patre invocato, quoniam tum praecipuus votorum locus est cum spei nullus est. Neque profugienti, cum potuisset, fera institerat, et procumbens ad arborem hiatu quo terruerat miserationem quaerebat. Os morsu avidiore inhaeserat dentibus cruciabatque inedia, non tantum poena in ipsis eius telis, suspectantem ac velut mutis precibus orantem, dum fortuita fides non est contra feram, multoque diutius miraculo

quam metu cessatur. Set degressus tandem (os) evellit praebenti (leoni) et
qua maxime opus esset adcommodanti; traduntque quamdiu navis ea in
litore steterit retulisse gratiam venatus adgerendo. . . . Ne miremur postea
vestigia hominum intellegi a feris, cum etiam auxilia ab uno animalium 25
sperent: cur enim non ad alia iere, aut unde medicas manus hominis sciunt?
Nisi forte vis malorum etiam feras omnia experiri cogit.

Vocabulary

ad + acc. near/nearby
adcommodo (1) to adjust/accommodate
adgero,-gerere,-gessi,-gestum to bring to (motion toward)
adulo,adulare to fawn on
animadverto,-vertere,-verti,-vertum to notice
animal,-alis n., living being/animal
arbor,arboris f., tree
argumentum,-i n., argument
attestor,attestari to attest/bear witness to
artifex,artificis skilled/creative
attonitus,-a,-um terrified
avidus,-a,-um eager/gluttonous
calamitas,calamitatis f., calamity/disaster/reverse of fortune
campus,-i m., open field
casus,-us m., occurrence
cessatur pass. impers., action is delayed/there is delay/hesitation
civilis,-e civil
clementia,-ae f., compassion
cogo,cogere,coegi,coactum to compel
conspicio,-spicere,-spexi,-spectum to observe/look at
contra + acc. in return/toward
credo,credere,credidi,creditum + dat. to entrust
cruciatus,-us m., pain/torment
crucio (1) to torture
currus,-us m., chariot
Cythereis,Cytheridis f., proper noun (a famous actress of the time)
damno (1) to condemn/impeach
defero,-ferre,-tuli,-latum to bring
degredior,-gredi,-gressus sum to go down/climb down
dens,dentis m., tooth
dimico (1) to contend/fight
dum adv., yet
Elpis,-is m., proper noun
evello,evellere,evelli to pull out
exemplum,-i n., example
extraho,-trahere,-traxi, -tractum to pull out
fera,-ae f., wild beast
feritas,feritatis f., ferocity
forte adv., by chance
fortuitus,-a,-um random
fuga,-ae f., flight
generosus,-a,-um noble
gratia,-ae f., thanks/gratitude
Hanno,Hannonis m., Hanno the Carthaginian general/son-in-law of Hamilcar Barca, the father of Hannibal
hiatus,-us m., open mouth
inedia,-ae f., starvation
ingenium,-i n., ability
inhaero,-haerere,-haesi,-haesum + dat. to stick
insto,instare,institi to give chase to/pursue
in tantum so completely/entirely
intellego,-legere,-lexi,-lectum to recognize
invoco (1) to invoke/call upon
iugum,-i n., yoke
iungo,iungere,iunxi,iunctum to harness
iuxta + acc. prep. near/nearby
lambo,lambere,lambi to lick
leo,leonis m., lion
Liber,-eri m., ancient Italian deity presiding over agriculture; later identified with Greek Bacchus
libertas,-atis f., freedom/free political status of a sovereign people
locus,-i m., moment/place

Marcus,-i Antonius,-i m., Mark Antony
male adv., wrongly
mansuefio,-fieri,-factus sum to be tame
medicus,-a,-um healing
Mentor,Mentoris m., proper noun
metus,-us m., fear (of what may happen)
mima,-ae f., actress
minax,minacis threatening
miraculum,-i n., amazement
miseratio,miserationis f., pity
monstrum,-i n., outrageousness/extreme wickedness
morsus,-us m., bite
mutus,-a,-um silent
obvius,-a,-um encountered on the road
oppono,-ponere,-posui,-positum to place opposite
opus est/esset impers., the task required/to be needed
oro (1) to plead
os,ossis n., bone
ostentum,-i n., intent/(something held up as an) example/foreshadowing
pavor,pavoris m., panic/terror
persuadeo,-suadere,-suasi,-suasum + dat. to convince/make pleasant
Pharsalius,-a,-um Pharsalian/of Pharsalia, an area in Greece
pictura,-ae f., painting
Poenus,-a,-um Carthaginian
postea adv., afterward/thereafter
praebeo,praebere,praebui,praebitum to offer/hold out
praecipuus,-a,-um special/preeminent
prex,precis f., prayer
procumbo,-cumbere,-cubi,-cubitum to lie down
prodigium,-i n., portent/ominous sign
profugio,-fugere,-fugi to escape
qua adv., in which way/where
quamdiu interrog./rel. adj., how long; conj., as long as
quoniam conj., inasmuch as/in view of the fact that
refero,-ferre,-ttuli,-latum to return
refugio,-fugere,-fugi to run away/take flight
Samius,-a,-um of Samos/Samian
significo,significare to indicate/signify
spiritus,-us m., spirit
subdo,subdere,subdidi,subditum to subdue/break (an animal)
subeo,-ire,-ii,-itum to go under
super adv., beyond
suppliciter adv., humbly
surculus,-i m., thorn
suspecto (1) to look up
Syracusanus,-a,-um Syracusan/of Syracuse
telum,-i n., splinter
testor,testari,testatus sum to attest
tracto (1) to lead
tumor,tumoris m., swelling
undique adv., everywhere/on all sides
vehor,veheri,vectus sum to ride
velut as/as if
venatus,-us m., catch/hunt
vero adv., in truth/to be sure
vestigium,-i n., track/footprint
volutans,volutantis rolling about
votum,-i n., prayer/vow
vulnus,vulneris n., wound

Wolves and Werewolves

Grammar Review

eo,ire,ii,itum	p. 132
idem,eadem,idem	p. 146
Infinitives of Indirect Statement	p. 131
Subjunctive Indirect Questions	p. 139

NB:	*ad praesens*	for the time being/temporarily
	habeo,habere,habui,habitum	to classify
	in + abl.	prep., among
	in tantum	so much/entirely
	per + acc.	prep., for
	quo?	Interrog., how far?

Sentences

1. Debemus existimare confidenter esse falsum homines in lupos verti rursusque restitui sibi aut debemus credere omnia fabulosa quae tot saeculis conperimus

2. Homines credunt lupos in Italia esse noxios hominibus quos contemplentur priores. Ista fama volgo infixa est in tantum ut in maledictis versipelles habeat.

3. Homo ex gente Anthi cuiusdam lectus sorte familiae ducitur ad quoddam stagnum. Vestitu in quercu suspenso, tranat atque abit in desertum locum ubi transfiguratur in lupum.

4. Ille transfiguratus per annos novem congregatur cum ceteris eiusdem generis. Si hominibus se abstinet, post novem annos rursus tranat idem stagnum et reciperat effigiemque etiam eandem vestem!

Translation

Sed in Italia quoque creditur luporum visus esse noxius, vocemque homini quem priores contemplentur adimere ad praesens. Inertes hos parvosque Africa et Aegyptus gignunt, asperos trucesque frigidior plaga. Homines in lupos verti rursusque restitui sibi falsum esse confidenter existimare debemus aut credere omnia quae fabulosa tot saeculis conperimus; unde 5
tamen ista volgo infixa sit fama in tantum ut in maledictis versipelles habeat indicabitur. Euanthes inter auctores Graeciae non spretus scribit Arcadas tradere ex gente Anthi cuiusdam sorte familiae lectum ad stagnum quoddam regionis eius duci vestituque in quercu suspenso tranare atque abire in deserta transfigurarique in lupum et cum ceteris eiusdem generis congregari 10
per annos IX; quo in tempore si homine se abstinuerit, reverti ad idem stagnum et, cum tranaverit, effigiem recipere, ad pristinum habitum addito novem annorum senio, addit quoque fabulosius eandem reciperare vestem! Mirum est quo procedat Graeca credulitas: nullum tam inpudens mendacium est ut teste careat. . . . 15

Vocabulary

abstineo,-tinere,-tinui,-tentum + abl. to hold back from/abstain from
addo,addere,addidi,additum to add
adimo,-imere,-emi,-emptum + dat. to take away from
Aegyptus,-i f., Egypt
Africa,-ae f., Africa
Anthus,-i m., Anthus
Arcades,-um m. pl., (Arcadas acc. pl.) Arcadians/ people of Arcadia
asper,aspera,asperum savage
confidenter adv., confidently
congrego (1) to assemble
conperio,-perire,-peri,-pertum to learn for a certainty
contemplor,contemplari to observe
credulitas,credulitatis f., credulity/gullibility
desertus,-a,-um desolate/deserted
effigies,-ei f., human likeness/form
Euanthes,-is m., Euanthes, an ancient writer

existimo (1) to regard/deem
fabulosus,-a,-um incredible
falsus,-a,-um false
fama,-ae f., rumor/hearsay
familia,-ae f., family
frigidus,-a,-um cold
gigno,gignere,genui,genitum to produce
habitus,-us m., appearance
indico (1) to reveal/indicate
iners,inertis feeble/weak
infigo,infigere,infixi,infixum to fix in the mind/ implant in the mind
inpudens,inprudentis shameless/outrageous
lupus,-i m., wolf
maledictum,-in curse/taunt
mendacium,-i n., lie
mirus,-a,-um amazing
noxius,-a,-um harmful
plaga,-ae f., region
prior,prioris before being seen first
pristinus,-a,-um former/earlier
procedo,-cedere,-cessi,-cessum to proceed/go
quercus,-us f., oak tree
quidam,quaedam,quoddam a certain
quoque adv., even
recipero (1) to regain/recover
regio,regionis f., region
restituo,-stituere,-stitui, -stitutum to restore
revertor,reverti,reverus sum to return
rursus adv., back/again
saeculum,-i n., century/age
senium,-i n., old age/aging
sors,sortis f., casting of lots
sperno,spernere,sprevi,spretum to scorn
stagnum,-i n., swamp
suspendo,-pendere,-pendi,-pensum to hang
testis,testis c., witness
trano (1) to swim across
transfiguro (1) to transform
trux, trucis fierce
versipellis,-is m., one who can change into different forms, e.g, a werewolf
vestis,vestis f., clothing
vestitus,-us m., clothing
visus,-us m., sight
volgus,-i n., common people
vox,vocis f., voice

The Dolphin, Its Habits, Susceptibility to Music, and Cases of Tame Dolphins

Grammar Review

Conditional Subjunctives	p. 139
Gerundives	p. 131
Gerundives of Purpose	

New Grammar

Alternative forms of the imperfect subjunctive of *sum,esse,fui,futurus*:

essem	*essemus*		***forem***	*(essemus)*
esses	*essetis*	=	***fores***	*(essetis)*
esset	*essent*		***foret***	***forent***

Ablatives of comparison occur with comparatives and are translated as *than.*

*Delphinus est ocior **volucre**, acrior **telo**.*

The Dolphin is faster **than a bird**, quicker **than a javelin**.

Occasionally the ablative case is used for duration of time

tricenis diebus	=	for thirty days
pluris annis	=	for several years

Gerundives (future active participles) are regularly used to express purpose.

Delphinus praebebat **puero ascensuro** dorsum.

The dolphin offered his back **for the boy to mount**.

NB:			
	acer,acris,acre		quick/fast
	amicus,-a,-um		friendly/inclined to
	causa,-ae		f., condition
	diutius		comp. adv., for so long
	in + acc.		prep. for
	iter,itineris		*n.,* journey
	ni	=	*nisi*
	non tantum . . . (sed) verum		not only . . . (but) also
	set	=	*sed*
	si		conj., since

Sentences

1. Nisi os delphini multum infra rostrum foret, nullus piscium celeritatem eius evaderet. Nam cum delphini fame conciti sint, in vada ima pisces sequuntur.

2. Vagantur fere coniugia, pariunt catulos decimo mense aestivo tempore, interim binos. Nutriunt catulos uberibus, sicut ballaena et gestant fetus infirmos infantia. Diu comitantur adultos magna erga partum caritate.

3. Haec historia traditur ab multis auctoribus. Quidam puer itans ex Baiano Puteolos in ludum litterarium inclamabat delphino invecto lacum Lucrinum. Saepius hunc delphinum appellatum nomine simonis adlexerat fragmentis panis quem ob iter ferebat.

4. Delphinus inclamatus a puero pastus e manu advolebat et condens aculeos pinnae velut in vagina, praebebat dorsum puero ascensuro. Plures annos delphinus ferebat puerum per magnum aequor ad ludum Puteolis simili modo revehens.

5. Delphinus hunc puerum miro amore dilexit. Puero extincto morbo, subinde delphinus consuetum locum ventitabat tristis et maerenti similis. Denique delphinus ipse quoque expiravit desiderio, quod nemo dubitabat.

Translation

Velocissimum omnium animalium, non solum marinorum, est delphinus ocior volucre, acrior telo, ac nisi multum infra rostrum os illi foret medio paene in ventre, nullus piscium celeritatem eius evaderet. Sed adfert moram providentia naturae, quia nisi resupini atque conversi non corripiunt. Quae causa praecipue velocitatem eorum ostendit: nam cum fame conciti fugientem in vada ima persecuti piscem diutius spiritum continuere ut arcu missi ad respirandum emicant; tantaque vi exsiliunt ut plerumque vela navium transvolent. Vagantur fere coniugia, pariunt catulos decimo mense aestivo tempore, interim et binos. Nutriunt uberibus, sicut ballaena, atque etiam gestant fetus infantia infirmos; quin et adultos diu comitantur magna erga partum caritate. Adolescunt celeriter, x annis putantur ad summam magnitudinem pervenire. Vivunt et tricenis, quod cognitum praecisa cauda in experimentum. Abduntur tricenis diebus circa canis ortum occultanturque incognito modo, quod eo magis mirum est si spirare in aqua non queunt. . . .

Delphinus non homini tantum amicum animal verum et musicae arti, mulcetur symphoniae cantu set praecipue hydrauli sono. Hominem non expavescit ut alienum, obviam navigiis venit, adludit exultans, certat etiam et quamvis plena praeterit vela. Divo Augusto principe Lucrinum lacum invectus pauperis cuiusdam puerum ex Baiano Puteolos in ludum litterarium itantem, cum meridiano immorans appellatum eum simonis nomine saepius fragmentis panis quem ob iter ferebat adlexisset, miro amore dilexit—pigeret referre ni res Maecenatis et Fabiani et Flavi Alfii multorumque esset litteris mandata, — quocumque diei tempore inclamatus a puero quamvis occultus atque abditus ex imo advolabat pastusque e manu praebebat ascensuro dorsum, pinnae aculeos velut vagina condens, 25 receptumque Puteolos per magnum aequor in ludum ferebat simili modo revehens pluribus annis, donec morbo extincto puero subinde ad consuetum locum ventitans tristis et maerenti similis ipse quoque, quod nemo dubitaret, desiderio expiravit.

Vocabulary

abdo,abdere,abdidi,abditum to go into hiding/hide from view
aculeus,-i m., point
adfero,adferre,attuli,allatum to carry/bring
adlicio,-licere,-lexi,-lectum to entice
adludo,-lere,-lusi,-lusum to play
adolesco,adolescere,adolevi to grow up
adulo,adulare to fawn
adultus,-a,-um grown/adult
advelo (1) to veil/hide
advolo (1) + acc. to hasten/fly to
aequor,-oris n., sea
aestivus,-a,-um (relating to) the summer
alienus,-a,-um strange/unfamiliar
amicus,-a,-um friendly/inclined to
amor,amoris m., affection
arcus,-us m., bow
ascendo,ascendere,ascendi,ascensum to ride/mount
Augustus,-i m., the first Roman emperor
ballaena,-ae f., whale
Baianum,-i n., the region of Baiae, on the bay of Naples
bini,-ae,-a two at a time
canis,-is m., Dog Star/Canis Major
cantus,-us m., song/melody
caritas,-atis f., affection
catulus,-i m., young animal/calf
cauda,-ae f., the tail of an animal
celeritas,-atis f., quickness/swiftness
certo (1) to vie with/compete
circa + acc. acc. prep. around
comitor (1) to accompany
concieo,conciere,concivi,concitum to stir up
condo,condere,condidi,conditum to fold away/store
coniugium,-i n., pair
consuetus,-a,-um accustomed/customary
conversio,-onis f., turning around
conversus,-a,-um upside down/turned over
corripio,corripere,corripui,correptum to attack/seize
delphinus,-i m., dolphin
desiderium,-i n., longing
diligo,diligere,dilexi,dilectum to love
donec adv., up to the time when/until
dorsum,-i n., back
emico,emicare,emicui,emicatum to spring forth/shoot up
exsilio,exsilire,exsilui to leap out
evado,evadere,evasi,evasum to escape
expavesco,expavescere,expavi + acc. acc. to show fear toward/be afraid of
experimentum,-i n., proof from experience
expiro (1) to expire/die
exsilio,exsilire,exsilui to leap out/up
extinguo,extinguere,extinxi,extinctum to kill
exulto (1) to race
Fabianus,-i (Papirius) m., a philosopher and teacher of the younger Seneca

fames,-is f., hunger
fere adv., generally/usually
fetus,-us m., newly delivered infant
Flavius,-i Alfius,-i m., possibly Flavius Alfius Avitus, a Latin poet of the late 1st century B.C.
fragmentum,-i n., piece/bit
gesto (1) to carry/bear about
hydraulus,-i m., water organ
immoror,immorari to stay/remain/delay
imus,-a,-um lowest/deepest
inclamo (1) to shout for/call
incognitus,-a,-um unknown
infantia,-ae f., infancy
infirmus,-a,-um weak/feeble
infra adv., below
interim adv., sometimes
inveho,invehere,imvexi,invectum to bring in
ito,itare,itavi to be in the habit of going
lacus,-us m., lake
litterarius,-a,-um relating to reading and writing
Lucrinus,-i m., a lake on the coast of Campania
ludus,-i m., school
Maecenas,-atis m., literary patron and friend of Augustus's; he was entrusted with the management of Rome and Italy
maereo,maerere to grieve/mourn
magnitudo,-inis f., size
mando (1) to commit to writing
marinus,-a,-um marine
mensis,-is m., month
meridianus,-a,-um midday
mirus,-a,-um astonishing/amazing
morbus,-i m., disease/sickness
mulceo,mulcere,mulsi,mulsum to charm
musica,-ae f., music
navigium,-i n., ship
nutrio,nutrire to suckle
obviam + dat. adv., to meet
ocior,ocius swifter/quicker
occultus,-a,-um concealed
occulto (1) to hide
ortus,-us m., the rising of a heavenly body/star
os,oris n., mouth
paene adv., almost
panis,-is m., bread
pario,parere,peperi,partum to bear
partus,-us m., offspring
pasco,pascere,pavi,pastum to feed
persequor,-sequi,-secutus sum to pursue
pervenio,-venire,-veni,-ventum to reach
piget,pigere,piguit,pigitum est impers., it causes shame/disgusts
pinna,-ae f., fin
piscis,-is m., fish
plenus,-a,-um full
plerumque adv., on many occasions/often
praebeo,-bere,-bui,-bitum to offer
praecido,-cidere,-cidi,-cisum to cut off
praecipue adv., especially
praetereo,-ire,-ivi,-itum to go by/pass
princeps,-ipis m., principate (office of head of state); title taken by Augustus
providentia,-ae f., foresight
Puteoli,-orum m. pl., a coastal town near Naples, now Pozzuoli
quamvis adv., however much/although
queo,quire,quivi,quitum to be able
quin adv., in fact
quicumque,quaecumque,quodcumque whoever/whatever
quidam,quaedam,quoddam a certain
refero,-ferre,-ttuli,-latum to repeat
respiro (1) to take a breath
resupinus,-a,-um on the back
reveho,-vehere,-vexi,-vectum to carry back
rostrum,-i n., snout
sicut adv., just as
simo,simonis snubnose (colloquial generic name given to dolphins)
sonus,-us m., sound
spiritus,-us m., breath
spiro (1) to breathe
symphonia,-ae f., a group of singers
subinde adv., repeatedly
transvolo (1) to fly over
triceni,-ae,-a thirty
tristis,-e sorrowful/sad
uber,-eris n., breast/teat
vadum,-i n., shallow place (in the sea)
vagina,-ae f., sheath/case
vagor,vagari,vagatus sum to roam
velocitas,-atis f., quickness/velocity
velox,-ocis swift
velum,-i n., sail
velut adv., as if
venter,-tris m., belly/stomach
ventito (1) to come often
volucris,volucris f., bird

Pearls; Cleopatra's Pearls and Her Wager with Antony

Grammar Review

New Grammar

alter,altera,alterum (one of the two/the other) is a 1st–2nd-declension adjective with irregular genitive and dative singular forms.

Nom.	alter
Gen.	alter**ius**
Dat.	alter**i**
Acc.	alterum
Abl.	altero

Roman coinage

as,assis

m, a Roman coin originally consisting of a pound of copper. In the third century the *as* was gradually reduced to half its value, and silver coins were introduced.

sestertius,-i

m, a sesterce was a Roman silver coin worth two and a half *asses.* HS is the abbreviation for *sestertius.*

centeni,-ae,-a a distributive numeral, 100 of each of something. After a distributive number the genitive plural is is required.

cetena milia sestertium = 100,000 sesterces

centiens

numeral adverb, 100 times; numeral adverbs are used with *mille* to express higher numbers.

centiens HS = centiens (centena milia) sesterium = 10 million sesterces

Neuter nouns with a nominative ending in *–ium* often have a genitive singular ending of ***–i*** instead of *–ii:*

pretium,preti n., worth/price

Nom.	pretium
Gen.	pret**i**
Dat.	pretio
Acc.	pretium
Abl.	pretio

NB:

alias	adv., otherwise
cum maxime	especially/exceedingly
in tantum	so much/so entirely
longus,-a,-um	spacious
tam	adv., so far
tantum	adv., only

Sentences

1. Margaritae ergo principium locum columenque omnium rerum preti tenent.
2. Non est dubium atteri usu; et mutare indiligentia colorem. Dos in candore, magnitudine, orbe, levore, pondere, haut rebus promptis in tantum ut nulli duo uniones reperiantur indiscreti.
3. Duo maximi uniones fuere per omne aevum et Cleopatra, novissima Aegypti reginarum, utrum possedit, uniones per manus orientis regum sibi traditos.
4. Haec Cleopatra, cum Antonius cotidie exquisitis epulis saginaretur, obtrectans omnem lautitiam apparatumque eius, eo quaerente quid magnificentiae adstrui posset—respondit se centiens HS una cena absumpturam esse.
5. Sponsionibus factis, postero die quo iudicium agebatur, Cleopatra apposuit Antonio, inridenti et expostulanti de computatione, alias magnificam cenam sed cotidianam, ne dies periret.
6. Ex praecepto ministri, ante eam tantum vas aceti posuere, cuius asperitas vis-que margaritas in tabem resolvit. Itaque Antonio expectante quidnam esset actura, detraxit alterum unionem ac mersit, ac liquefactum obsorbuit.
7. L. Plancus, iudex sponsionis eius, manum alteri unioni iniecit, Cleopatra quoque parante eum in simili modo absumere, et Antonium victum omine rato pronuntiavit.

Chapter XII

Translation

Principium ergo columenque omnium rerum preti margaritae tenent. Indicus maxime has mittit oceanus inter illas beluas tales tantasque quas diximus per tot maria venientes tam longo terrarum tractu e tantis solis ardoribus. Atque Indis quoque in insulas petuntur et admodum paucas: fertilissima est Taprobane et Stoidis, ut diximus in circuitu mundi, item Perimula promunturium Indiae; praecipue autem laudantur circa Arabiam in Persico sinu maris Rubri . . .

Usu atteri non dubium est, coloremque indiligentia mutare. Dos omnis in candore, magnitudine, orbe, levore, pondere, haut promptis rebus in tantum ut nulli duo reperiantur indiscreti: unde nomen unionum Romanae scilicet imposuere deliciae, nam id apud Graecos non est, nec apud barbaros quidem, inventores rei eius aliud quam margaritae. Et in candore ipso magna differentia; clarior in Rubro mari repertis, in Indico specularium lapidum squamas adsimulant, alias magnitudine praecellentes . . .

. . . Duo fuere maximi uniones per omne aevum; utrumque possedit Cleopatra Aegypti reginarum novissima per manus orientis regum sibi traditos. Haec, cum exquisitis cotidie Antonius saginaretur epulis, superbo simul ac procaci fastu, ut regina meretrix, lautitiam eius apparatumque omnem obtrectans, quaerente eo quid adstrui magnificentiae posset respondit una se cena centiens HS absumpturam. Cupiebat discere Antonius, sed fieri posse non arbitrabatur. Ergo sponsionibus factis postero die, quo iudicium agebatur, magnificam alias cenam, ne dies periret, sed cotidianam, Antonio apposuit inridenti computationemque expostulanti. At illa corollarium id esse, et consummaturam eam cenam taxationem confirmans solamque se centiens HS cenaturam, inferri mensam secundam iussit. Ex praecepto 25 ministri unum tantum vas ante eam posuere aceti, cuius asperitas visque in tabem margaritas resolvit. Gerebat auribus cum maxime singulare illud et vere unicum naturae opus. Itaque expectante Antonio quidnam esset actura detractum alterum mersit ac liquefactum obsorbuit. Iniecit alteri manum L. Plancus, iudex sponsionis eius, eum quoque parante simili modo absumere, 30 victumque Antonium pronuntiavit omine rato. . . .

Vocabulary

absum,-esse,-fui to be absent
absumo,-sumere,-sumpsi,-sumptum to consume
acetum,-i n., vinegar
admodum adv., quite/very
adsimulo (1) to resemble
adstruo,-struere,-strui,-stuctum to add to
aevum,-i n., time/history
Aegyptus-i m., Egypt
alius,-a,-um other
alter,altera,alterum one of the two/the other
Antonius,-i m., Marc Antony
apparatus,-us m., pomp/display
appono,apponere,apposui, appositum to serve
Arabia,-ae f., Arabia
arbitror,arbitrari,arbitratus sum to judge/ consider
ardor,-oris m., burning heat
asperitas,-atis f., harshness
attero,atterere,attriui,attritum to wear down
auris,-is f., ear
barbarus,-a,-um foreign
belua,-ae f., beast/wild animal
candor,-oris m., luster/brilliance
ceno (1) to dine
centiens HS 10 million sesterces
circa + acc. adv., around
circuitus,-us m., circuit/going
clarus,-a,-um bright
Cleopatra,-ae f., Cleopatra
color,-oris m., color
columen,-inis n., highest place/rank
computatio,-onis f., cost
confirmo (1) to assure/give assurance
consummo (1) to cost/sum/use up
corollarium,-i n., accompaniment
cotidianus,-a,-um every day/ordinary
cotidie adv., daily
deliciae,-arum f. pl., luxury
detraho,-trahere,-traxi,-tractum to detach/remove
dico,dicere,dixi,dictum to describe
differentia,-ae f., difference
dos,dotis f., quality/value
dubium,-i n., doubt
epulae,-arum f. pl., banquet/feasts
expecto (1) to wait for/await
expostulo (1) to complain/dispute
exquisitus,-a,-um exquisite/elaborate
fastus,-us m., haughtiness/arrogance
fertilis,-is productive/fertile
gero,gerere,gessi,gestum to wear

haut adv., not
impono,-ponere,-posui,-positum to place/put upon
Indi,-orum m. pl., inhabitants of India
India,-ae f., India
Indicus,-a,-um Indian
indiligentia,-ae f., lack of care/negligence
indiscretus,-a,-um indistinguishable
infero,inferre,intuli,inlatum to bring in
inicio,inicere,inieci,iniectum to put/place
inrideo,inridere,inrisi,inrisum to laugh
insula,-ae f., island
inventor,-oris m., discoverer
item adv., similarly/in the same manner
iudex,-icis m., judge
iudicium,-i n., judgment/decision
lapis,-idis m., stone
lautitia,-ae f., luxury
levor,-oris smoothness/evenness
liquefacio,-facere,-feci,-factum to dissolve/make liquid
longus,-a,-um vast/spacious
Lucius,-i Plancus,-i m., Lucius Munatius Plancus was Julius Caesar's officer during the conquest of Gaul and the civil war against Pompey. When Caesar was assassinated on March 15, 44 B.C., Plancus was the proconsul of Gallia Comata. But the following year the turned to Mark Antony, and he held the consulship with Marcus Aemilius Lepidus in 42 B.C. He became proconsul of Asia in about 40 B.C. and ca. 36 B.C. was proconsul of Syria. But when Antony's campaign against the Parthians failed, he chose to leave him and join Octavian.
magnificentia,-ae f., magnificence/ majesty
magnitudo,-inis f., magnitude/weight/size
magnificus,-a,-um great
margarita,-ae f., a pearl
mensa,-ae f., course (in a meal)
meretrix,meretricis f., harlot
merso (1) to immerse
minister,-tri m., servant
novissimus,-a,-um the last
obsorbeo,-sorbere,-sorbui to swallow
obtrecto (1) to criticize/belittle
oceanus,-i m., occan
omen,-inis n., prophecy
orbis,-is m., roundness
oriens,-ntis m., the east
Perimula,-ae f., name for the promontory of India
pereo,perire,perrii,peritum to be wasted/go to waste
Persicus,-a,-um Persian
pondus,-eris n., weight
possideo,-sidere,-sedi,-sessum to own/possess
posterus,-a,-um next/following
praecellens,-ntis surpassing/exceeding
praeceptum,-i n., previous instruction
praecipue adv., especially
pretium,-i n., worth/price
principius,-a,-um first/foremost
procax,-acis insolent/impudent
promptus,-a,-um visible/apparent
promunturium,-i n., headland/promontory
pronuntio (1) to pronounce/declare
quisnam,quidnam who/what
ratus,-a,-um fulfilled/granted fulfillment
regina,-ae f., queen
resolvo,-solvere,-solvi,-solutum to dissolve
ruber,rubra,rubrum red
sagino (1) to fatten/cram/stuff full
scilicet naturally/obviously
singularis,-e remarkable
sinus,-us m., gulf
solus,-a,-um alone
specularis,-e translucent
sponsio,-onis f., a bet
squama,-ae f., flake/scale
Stoidis,-is f., island off the coast of India
superbus,-a,-um proud/haughty
tabes,-is f., liquid (resulting from dissolving)
talis,-e remarkable/of such a kind
Taprobane,-es f., Ceylon/Sri Lanka
taxatio,-onis f., evaluation/assessment
tot indecl., this many/that many
tractus,-us m., expanse (of land)/extent
unicus,-a,-um sole/unique
unio,unire,unii,unitum to unite/combine into one
unio,-onis m., unique gem/a pearl
usus,-us m., use
uterque,utraque,utrumque both
vas,vasis n., container/vessel
vere adv., truly

Scarlet and Purple Cloth: Luxury Items as Costly as Pearls

Grammar Review

New Grammar

The indefinite pronoun *quis/quid* (anyone/anything or someone/something) has an alternate dative and ablative plural form:

	m. pl.	f. pl.	n. pl.
Nom.	*qui*	*quae*	*quae*
Gen.	*quorum*	*quarum*	*quorum*
Dat	*quibus/**quis***	*quibus/**quis***	*quibus/**quis***
Acc.	*quos*	*quas*	*quae*
Abl.	*quibus/**quis***	*quibus/**quis***	*quibus/**quis***

Potential subjunctive expressing a possibility:

*Insania purpurae **sit** excusata.*

The insanity for purple **may be** excused.

A clause introduced by a relative pronoun or relative adverb may express a condition.

*(vestis) dibapha tunc dicebatur **quae bis tincta esset***

(a garment) then was called double dyed **which would have been dyed twice**

Pliny often uses the ablative case to denote duration of time:

annis septenis = **for seven years**

NB:		
	cos. =	*consul*
	fasces securesque	f., rods and axes, i.e., symbols of Roman supremacy
	facio,facere,feci,factum	to secure/make safe
	gravis,-is	offensive/unpleasant
	hīc	adv., here
	in + acc.	prep. for
	in libras	per pound
	ius,iuris	n., juice
	plurimum	adv., at most
	pro indiviso	equally/in equal proportion
	qua propter?	Interrog., wherefore? why?
	satis constat with acc. + inf.	3rd impers., it is sufficiently established/generally agreed
	tanto—quanto	by so much—by how much

Special types of the *toga*

toga praetexta	a toga with a purple border worn by magistrates and freeborn children
toga virilis/toga pura	the plain undyed woolen toga assumed by freeborn young men on reaching maturity, generally 14 to 18 years old
toga candida	a toga made of cloth filled with chalk, worn by candidates for office

Sentences

1. Purpurae annis plurimum septenis vivunt. Verno tempore congregantur, mutuoque attritu lentorem cuiusdam cerae salivant.

2. Purpurae florem illum expetitum tinguendis vestibus in mediis faucibus habent. Hic est candida vena unde pretiosus ille liquor nigrantis rosae coloris bibitur.

3. Maioribus purpuris vivas capere contendunt et detracta concha auferunt, sed minoribus purpuris cum testa vivas frangunt, ita demum eum liquorem pretiosum exspuentes.

4. Praecipuus est liquor Tyri Asiae, Meninge Africae, et Gaetulo litore oceani, in Laconica Europae. Fasces securesque Romanae huic viam faciunt.

5. Idem color pro maiestate pueritiae est; ab equite curiam distinguit, dis placandis advocatur, omnemque vestem inluminat, in triumphali auro miscetur.

6. Nepos Cornelius, qui divi Augusti principatu obiit, inquit: "Me iuvene, violacea purpura vigebat, cuius libra denariis centum venibat, nec multo post rubra Tarentina. Dibapha Tyria purpura in libras denariis mille non poterat emi. Lentulus Spinther, aedilis curulis primus usus hac in toga praetexta, improbabatur, sed quis iam triclinaria qua purpura non facit?"

7. Praeter ius temperatur aqua et pro indiviso humani potus excremento; et dimidia medicamina adduntur. Ille pallor sic laudatus gignitur saturitate fraudata tantoque color dilutior quanto magis vellera esuriunt.

Chapter XIII

Translation

Purpurae vivunt annis plurimum septenis. Latent sicut murices circa canis ortum tricenis diebus. Congregantur verno tempore, mutuoque attritu lentorem cuiusdam cerae salivant. Simili modo et murices, sed purpurae florem illum tinguendis expetitum vestibus in mediis habent faucibus: Liquoris hic minimi est candida vena unde pretiosus ille bibitur, nigrantis 5 rosae colore sublucens; reliquum corpus sterile. Vivas capere contendunt, quia cum vita sucum eum evomunt; et maioribus quidem purpuris detracta concha auferunt, minores cum testa vivas frangunt, ita demum eum exspuentes. Tyri praecipuus hic Asiae, Meninge Africae et Gaetulo litore oceani, in Laconica Europae. Fasces huic securesque Romanae viam faciunt, 10 idemque pro maiestate pueritiae est; distinguit ab equite curiam, dis advocatur placandis, omnemque vestem inluminat, in triumphali miscetur auro. Quapropter excusata et purpurae sit insania; sed unde conchyliis pretia, quis virus grave in fuco, color austerus in glauco et irascenti similis mari? . . .

Purpurae usum Romae semper fuisse video, sed Romulo in trabea: 15 nam toga praetexta et latiore clavo Tullum Hostilium e regibus primum usum Etruscis devictis satis constat. Nepos Cornelius, qui divi Augusti principatu obiit: "Me," inquit, "iuvene violacea purpura vigebat, cuius libra denariis centum venibat, nec multo post rubra Tarentina. Huic successit dibapha Tyria, quae in libras denariis mille non poterat emi. Hac P. Lentulus 20 Spinther aedilis curulis primus in praetexta usus improbabatur, qua purpura quis non iam," inquit, "triclinaria facit?" Spinther aedilis fuit urbis conditae anno DCXCI Cicerone cos, dibapha tunc dicebatur quae bis tincta esset, veluti magnifico impendio, qualiter nunc omnes paene commodiores purpurae tinguuntur. 25

In conchyliata veste cetera eadem sine bucino, praeterque ius temperatur aqua et pro indiviso humani potus excremento; dimidia et medicamina adduntur. Sic gignitur laudatus ille pallor saturitate fraudata tantoque dilutior quanto magis vellera esuriunt.

Vocabulary

addo,addere,addidi,additum to add
advoco (1) to summon
aedilis,-is m., aedile, an elected official in Republican Rome
Africa,-ae f., Roman Africa
aqua,-ae f., water
attritus,-us m., rubbing/grinding
aufero,auferre,abstuli,ablatum to destroy
aurum,auri n., gold
austerus,-a,-um gloomy
bibo,bibere,bibi,bibitum to drain
bis adv., twice
bucinum,-i n., whelk (trumpet-shaped shellfish producing high-quality purple dye)
candidus,-a,-um shining white
canis,-is m., the dog star present in the sky in the spring
centeni,-ae,-a a hundred (at a time)
cera,-ae f., wax
circa + acc. prep., around the time of/close to the time of
clavus,-i m., a stripe of purple on the tunic worn by senators (wide stripe) and equites (narrow)
color,coloris m., hue/color
commodus,-a,-um satisfactory
concha,-ae f., shell
conchyliatus,-a,-um dyed with ordinary purple
conchylium,-i n., ordinary purple shellfish (i.e., shellfish producing ordinary purple dye)
conditus,-a,-um founded
congrego (1) to collect together
constat impers., it is established/well known
contendo,-tendere,-tendi,-tentum to strive
curulis,curulis of curile rank
curia,-ae f., the Senate
demum adv., and not before/at last
denarius,-i m., Roman silver coin equivalent to 10 asses (*as,assis* Roman coin of lowest unit value)
detraho,-trahere,-traxi,-tractum to strip off
devinco,-vincere,-vici,-victum to conquer
dibaphus,-a,-um double dyed
dilutus,-a,-um weakened/pale
dimidius,-a,-um half
distinguo,-stingere,-stinxi,-stinctum to divide up
divus,-i Augustus,-i m., the deified Augustus
eques,-itis m., knight, a distinct social order between the Senate and the plebs
emo,emere,emi,emptum to buy
esurio,esurire,esurivi,esuritum to imbibe/soak up (*i.e.* vellera esuriunt . . . the skins are absorbent)
Etruscus,-a,-um Etruscan
Europa,-ae f., continent of Europe
evomo,evomere,evomui,evomitum to spew out/discharge
excrementum,-i n., excrement
excuso (1) to excuse
expeto,-petere,-petivi,-petitum to desire
exspuo,-spuere,-spui,-sputum to eject/emit/disgorge

fauces,faucium f. pl., throats
flos,floris m., luster/tint
frango,frangere,fregi,fractum to break/crush
fraudo (1) to leach/weaken
fucus,-i m., purple dye
Gaetulus,-a,-um Gaetulan/people from northwestern Africa
gigno,gignere,genui,genitum to cause/produce
glaucus,-a,-um bluish green
impendium,-i n., cost/expenditure
improbo (1) to criticize
inlumino (1) to light up
insania,-ae f., madness
irascens,-ntis angry
ius,iuris n., juice
iuvenis,-is m., youth
Laconica,-ae f., country of Sparta
lateo,latere,latui,latitum to lie hidden
latus,-a,-um broad/wide
lentor,-oris m., a viscous substance
Lentulus Spinther m., Publius Cornelius Lentulus Spinther first attained public office in 63 B.C. (the year of Cicero's consulship) when he was voted curule aedile. In that office, Spinther assisted Cicero in the suppression of the Catiline conspiracy, and he also disginguished himself by the splendor of the games he provided (though the royal purple stripe he used on his toga is said to have offended many Romans to whom purple was connected with royalty and therefore anathema to a good Roman).
libra,-ae f., a unit of weight in ancient Rome equivalent to about 12 ounces
liquor,liquoris m., liquid/fluid
maiestas,-atis f., dignity
magnificus,-a,-um lavish/extravagant
medicamen,-inis n., dye
medius,-a,-um middle
Meninx,Meningis f., proper noun, town in Africa
misceo,miscere,miscui,mixtum to combine/mix
murex,muricis m., shellfish from which purple was taken
mutuus,-a,-um mutual/reciprocal
Nepos,-otis Cornelius,-i m., Cornelius Nepos (ca. 100–24 B.C.) was a Roman biographer. He was a friend of Catullus, who dedicates his poems to him (1.3), Cicero, and Titus Pomponius Atticus. Eusebius places him in the fourth year of the reign of Augustus, when he supposedly began to attract critical acclaim as a writer. Pliny the Elder notes that he died in the reign of Augustus (Natural History IX.39, X.23).
nigrans,nigrantis dark
obeo,-ire,-ii,-itum to die
oceanus,-i m., the ocean
ortus,-us m., rising
paene adv., almost
pallor,-oris m., paleness
placo (1) to appease/placate
potus,-us m., drinking
praecipuus,-a,-um excellent/extraordinary
praeter adv., in addition
praetexta,-ae f., purple-bordered toga
pretiosus,-a,-um costly/precious
pretium,preti n., worth/price
primus,-a,-um first
principatus,-us m., principate/rule of a particular princeps
puertia,pueritiae f., boyhood
purpura,purpurae f., an expensive purple dyed cloth/the shellfish producing the most intense and valuable purple dye
qualiter adv., in this way/in which manner
quapropter rel. adv., on which account
quinquageni,-ae,-a fifty (each)
Romulus,-i n., founder of Rome
rosa,rosae f., rose
ruber,rubra,rubrum red
salivo (1) to exude/discharge
saturitas,-atis f., coloration (by dyeing)
septini,-ae,-a adv., seven (at a time)
sicut adv., just as
sterilis,sterile unproductive/useless
subluceo,-lucere,-lucui,-lucitum to glimmer
succedo,-cedere,-cessi,-cessum + dat. to follow
sucus,-i m., juice
Tarentinus,-a,-um Tarentine/connected with Tarentum (modern Taranto), a town in southern Italy
tempero (1) to temper/dilute
testa,-ae f., shell
tinguo,tinguere,tinxi,tinctum to dye
toga,-ae f., a toga was the formal outer garment worn by Roman men (see page 61 for official types of togas)
trabea,-ae f., cloak/a short purple or partly purple garment of Etruscan origin
triceni,-ae,-a thirty (at a time)
triclinaria,-ium n., covering for a dining couch/ couch cover
triumphalis,-e relating to a triumphal procession of a conquering general
Tullus,-i Hostilius,-i the third king of Rome
tunc adv., then

Tyrius,-a,-um Tyrian
Tyrus,Tyri f., Tyre, a Phoenician city
vellus,-eris n., wool fiber
veluti just as
vena,venae f., vein
veneo,venire,venii to be sold
vernus,-a,-um springtime
vestis,vestis f., garment
vigeo,vigere,vigui,vigetum to flourish/be popular
vilis,-e cheap
violaceus,-a,-um violet colored
virus,-i n., smell/odor
vivus,-a,-um alive/living

Perfumes, When Invented, Places of Origin, and Changes of Fashion

Grammar Review

Irregular Adverbs p. 148
Subjunctive Indirect Questions p. 139

New Grammar

The suffix ***–inus*** can be appended to the names of plants or other materials to form adjectives with the sense of *belonging to.*

iris,iridis f., the iris flower	*narcissus,-i* m., the narcissus flower
*ir**inus**,-a,-um* of the iris plant	*narciss**inus**,-a,-um* of the narcissus flower

Impersonal verb forms appear in 3rd-person singular; the subject is translated as ***it***.

convenit	**it** is fitting
iuvit (with acc. + inf.)	**it** pleases/delights
supplicabatur	**it** was worshipped
traditur	**it** is handed down

A subjunctive relative clause of characteristic may expression restriction or conditional stipulation, i.e., *as far as I know, as far as I have heard.*

Primum (unguentum) ***quod equidem inveniam*** . . .

The first perfume, indeed as far as I discover . . .

NB:		
	ad praesens	for the present
	alibi . . . alibi	here . . . there
	aliis. . .aliis	some . . . others
	auctoritas,-atis	f., popularity
	bonum,-i	n., blessing/boon/enjoyment
	gloria,-ae	f., renown/fame

iidem (idem,eadem,idem)	=	*eidem*
optinuere	=	*optinuerun*
scio, scire, scivi, scitum		to be cognizant/aware

Sentences

1. Hactenus silvae pretia in odoribus habent. Iuvit luxuriam miscere omnia ea et facere unum odorem e cunctis.
2. Persae invenere unguentum. Illi se madent ut extinguant virus natum inluvie. Alexander castris Darii expugnatis scrinium unguentorum in relicto apparatu cepit.
3. Patriae, suci, arbores et alia unguentis cognomina dederunt.
4. Convenit scire auctoritatem unguentorum mutatam esse et gloriam saepius transisse.
5. Iidem suci praevaluere alibi et degeneravere alibi.

Translation

Hactenus in odoribus habent pretia silvae, erantque parum per se mira singula, iuvitque luxuriam omnia ea miscere et e cunctis unum odorem facere: ita reperta sunt unguenta. Quis primus invenerit non traditur. Iliacis temporibus non erant, nec ture supplicabatur: cedri tantum et citri suorum fruticum et in sacris fumo convolutum nidorem verius quam odorem noverant, iam rosae suco reperto; nominatur enim hic quoque in olei laude. Unguentum Persarum gentis esse debet; illi madent eo et accersita commendatione inluvie natum virus extingunt. Primum, quod equidem inveniam, castris Darii regis expugnatis in reliquo eius apparatu Alexander cepit scrinium unguentorum. Postea voluptas eius a nostris quoque inter lautissima atque etiam honestissima vitae bona admissa est, honosque et ad defunctos pertinere coepit; quapropter plura de eo dicemus. Quae ex his non erunt fruticum ad praesens nominibus tantum indicabuntur, natura vero eorum suis reddetur locis.

Unguentis cognomina dedere aliis patriae, aliis suci, aliis arbores, aliis aliae causae; primumque id scire convenit, mutata auctoritate et saepius transisse gloriam: laudatissimum fuit antiquitus in Delo insula, postea Mendesium. Nec mixtura et conpositione tantum hoc accidit, sed iidem suci varie alibi atque alibi praevaluere aut degeneravere. Irinum Corinthi diu maxime placuit, postea Cyzici, simili modo rhodinum Phaselide, quam gloriam abstulere Neapolis, Capua, Praeneste. Crocinum Solis Ciliciae diu maxime laudatum est, mox Rhodi; oenanthinum in Cypro, post Adramytteo, amaracinum in Coo, postea eodem loco praelatum est melinum, cyprinum in Cypro, deinde in Aegypto, ubi Mendesium et metopium subito gratius factum est; mox haec abstulit Phoenice et cyprini laudem Aegypto reliquit. Panathenaicum suum Athenae perseveranter optinuere. Fuerat et pardalium in Tarso, cuius etiam conpositio et mixtura oblitterata est; narcissinum quoque ex flore narcisso desiit conponi. 25

Vocabulary

accersitus,-a,-um coming from another source/borrowed
admitto,-mittere,-misi,-missum to admit
Adramytteum,-i a city on the coast of Mysia in Asia Minor
Aegyptus,-i f., Egypt
Alexander,-dri m., Alexander the Great
alibi adv., elsewhere
amaracinum,-i n., marjoram perfume
antiquitus adv., long ago/from antiquity
apparatus,-us m., splendor/pomp
auctoritas,-atis f., popularity/approval
aufero,auferre,abstuli,ablatus to carry off/appropriate
Capua,-ae f., Capua, city of Campania
castra,-orum n. pl., military camp
cedrus,-i f., cedar tree
Cilicia,-ae f., Roman province in Southeast Asia Minor
citrus,-i f., citron tree
cognomen,-inis n., name
commendatio,-onis f., commendation/approval
conpono,-ponere,-posui,-positum to prepare/compound/make
conpositio,-onis f., a combination/composition
convenit 3rd impers., it is fitting
convolvo,-volvere,-volvi,-volutum to intertwine/wreathe
Coos,-i f., Cos, an island in the Dodecanese
Corinthus,-i f., Corinth
crocinum,-i n., saffron oil, from the crocus flower
cunctus,-a,-um all collectively/the whole
cyprinum,-i n., henna oil
Cyprus,-i m., Cyprus, island in the Aegean
Cyzicus,-i f., Cyzicus, a town on the south coast of Propontis of Asia
Darius,-i m., Darius, the Persian king
defunctus,-a,-um dead
degenero (1) to decline
Delos,-i f., Delos, an island in the Aegean Sea
desino,-sinere,desii,desitus + inf. to cease
equidem adv., indeed
expugno (1) to capture
extinguo,-tinguere,-tinxi,-tinctum to extinguish
flos,floris m., flower
frutex,-icis f., shrub
fumus,-i m., smoke
gloria,-ae f., renown/fame
gratus,-a,-um pleasing
hactenus adv., only so far
honestus,-a,-um honorable/worthy
honos,-oris m., tribute
iam adv., already/by this time
Iliacus,-a,-um Trojan
indico (1) to indicate
inluvies,-ei f., dirt
irinum,-i n., the iris scent
iuvit (with acc. + inf.) 3rd impers., it pleased/gratified
laus,laudis f., a praiseworthy quality
lautus,-a,-um luxurious/elegant
luxuria,-ae f., luxury/extravagance
madeo,madere,madui,maditum to soak/to be steeped in

melinum,-i n., quince-seed oil
Mendesius,-a,-um of Mendes, an Egyptian town
metopium,-i n., almond-oil scent
mirus,-a,-um extraordinary/amazing
misceo,miscere,miscui,mixtum to combine/mix together
mixtura,-ae f., mixture/blend
narcissinus,-a,-um of the narcissus flower
narcissus,-i m., narcissus (the flower)
Neapolis,-is f., Naples, in southern Italy
nidor,-oris m., reek/odor
nomino (1) to name/designate
nosco,noscere,novi,notum to be accquainted with/ familiar with
oblittero (1) to obliterate/lose
odor,-oris m., fragrance/scent
oenanthinus,-a,-um made from the flower of the wild vine (a plant having the scent of forming grapes, perhaps the dropwort)
oleum,-i n., olive oil
optineo,-tinere,-tinui,-tentum to maintain
Panathenaicus,-a,-um all-Athenian
pardalium,-i n., panther-scented perfume
parum adv., too little/not enough
Persa,-arum m. pl., the Persians
perserveranter adv., persistently
pertineo,-tinere,-tenui to apply/belong by right
Phaselis,-idis f., Phaeselis, a town on the coast of Lycia, an area of modern-day Turkey
Phoenice,-es f., Phoenicia, the coastal region of Syria
post/postea adv., afterward
praefero,-ferre,-tuli,-latum to prefer
Praeneste,-is n., town in southern Italy
praevaleo,praevalere,praevalui to gain supremacy/prevail
pretium,-i n., value/worth
primum adv., first
quapropter rel. adv., on which account
reddo,reddere,reddidi,redditum to give/render
reliquus,-a,-um remaining
reperio,reperire,repperi,repertum to invent/ discover
rhodinus,-a,-um made from roses
Rhodus,-i f., Rhodes, an island in the Greek Dodecanese
rosa,-ae f., a rose
sacra,-orum n. pl., sacred rites/worship
scrinium,-i n., box/case
silva,-ae f., forest
singuli,-ae,-a remarkable/one alone
Soli,-orum m. pl., Soli, a town in Cilicia
subito adv., suddenly
sucus,-i m., fragrance/essence/attar
supplicabatur impers., it was worshipped/prayed to the gods
tantum adv., only
traditur impers., it is handed down
Tarsus,-i f., Tarsus, a town in Cilicia
transeo,-ire,-ii,-itum to pass away
tus, turis n., frankincense
unguentum,-i n., perfume
varie adv., variously/changeably
vero conj., but indeed
virus,-i n., smell
voluptas,voluptatis f., pleasure

History of the Use of Paper: The Discovery of 181 B.C.

Grammar Review

idem, eadem, idem	p. 146
ipse, ipsa, ipsum	p. 144
Subjunctive Indirect Questions	p. 139

New Grammar

Abbreviations

SC = *Senatus Consultum* = a formal resolution of the Senate

Official identification denoted the father.

M.(arcus) Baebius Q.(uinto) filiius Tamphilus =
Marcus Baebius Tamphilus son to Quintus

P.(ublius) Cornelius L.(ucio) filius Cethegus =
Publius Cornelius Cethegus son to Lucius

The archaic form of the present passive infinitive ended in –***ier***.

*arbitror, arbitrar**ier**, arbitratus sum* = to reckon/think

The 3rd principal part of *sum,esse,**fui**,futurus* is sometimes used to form compound passive tenses; e.g., *sino,sinere,sivi,situm* (to bury)

Indicative:	Perfect Passive **situs fui**, etc.	Pluperfect Passive **situs fueram**, etc.	Future Perfect Passive **situs fuero**, etc.
Subjunctive:	Perfect Passive **situs fuerim**, etc.	Pluperfect Passive **situs fuissem,** etc	
Infinitive:	***situm,-am,-um fuisse***		

Ablative of attendant circumstance denotes the circumstances of an action or an event: *maiore etiamnum miraculo* a still greater wonder

Alternate plural forms for *is,ea,id*:

	m. pl.	f. pl.	n. pl.
Nom.	*ei,**ii,i***	*eae*	*ea*
Gen.	*eorum*	*earum*	*eorum*
Dat.	*eis,**iis,is***	*eis,**iis,is***	*eis,**iis,is***
Acc.	*eos*	*eas*	*ea*
Abl.	*eis,**iis,is***	*eis,**iis,is***	*eis,**iis,is***

Sentences

1. Cassius Hemina prodidit in eius quarto libro scribam Gnaeum Terentium, cum repastinantem suum agrum in Ianiculo, effodisse arcam in qua corpus Numae, qui Romae regnavit, situm fuisset.
2. Cassius dicit in eadem arca libros Numae repertos esse; hos libros fuisse e charta. Ea arca effodiebatur consulatu P. Cornelii Cethegi et M. Baebii Tamphili, ad quos DXXXV anni colliguntur a regno Numae.
3. Alii mirabantur quomodo illi libri possent durare; Terentius reddebat rationem: lapidem quadratum circiter in media arca fuisse; hunc lapidem vinctum esse candelis quoquoversus; in eo lapide insuper sitos fuisse III libros.
4. Antias dixit fuisse XII pontificales libros Latinos et XII libros scriptos in Graeco, continentes praecepta philosophiae.
5. Inter omnes vero convenit, Sibyllam adtulisse tres libros ad Tarquinium Superbum, et ex quibus ab Sibylla ipsa duo cremati sint, et tertius cum Capitolio Sullanis temporibus.

Translation

Ingentia exempla contra M. Varronis sententiam de chartis reperiuntur. Namque Cassius Hemina, vetustissimus auctor annalium, quarto eorum libro prodidit Cn. Terentium scribam agrum suum in Ianiculo repastinantem effodisse arcam in qua Numa qui Romae regnavit situs fuisset; in eadem libros eius repertos P. Cornelio L. filio Cethego, M. Baebio Q. filio 5
Tamphilo cos. ad quos a regno Numae colliguntur anni DXXXV; hos fuisse e charta, maiore etiamnum miraculo, quod infossi duraverint—quapropter in re tanta ipsius Heminae verba ponam: 'Mirabantur alii quomodo illi libri durare possent; ille ita rationem reddebat: lapidem fuisse quadratum circiter in media arca vinctum candelis quoquoversus; in eo lapide insuper libros 10
III sitos fuisse: se propterea arbitrarier non computruisse; et libros citratos fuisse: propterea arbitrarier tineas non tetigisse. In iis libris scriptae erant philosophiae Pythagoricae—eosque combustos a Q. Petilio praetore [quia philosophiae scripta essent]. Hoc idem tradit Piso censorius primo commentariorum, sed libros septem iuris pontificii, totidem Pythagoricos 15
fuisse; Tuditanus tertio decumo Numae decretorum libros XII fuisse; ipse Varro humanarum antiquitatum VII, Antias secundo libros fuisse XII pontificales Latinos, totidem Graecos praecepta philosophiae continentes; idem tertio et SC. ponit quo comburi eos placuerit. Inter omnes vero convenit Sibyllam ad Tarquinium Superbum tres libros adtulisse, ex quibus 20
sint duo cremati ab ipsa, tertius cum Capitolio Sullanis temporibus . . .'

Vocabulary

adfero,adferre,attuli,allatum to bring
annales,-ium m. pl., historical compilations
Antias Valerius m., Sullan annalist, wrote a history of Rome from the origins to his own time
Antiquitates,-um f. pl., Varro's books on the topic of human affairs
arca, -ae f., a coffer/coffin
candela, -ae f., waxed cord
Capitolium, -i n., the temple to Jupiter on the Capitoline Hill in Rome
Cassius Hemina m., the first Latin annalist, he treated Roman history from early Italian times to 146 B.C.
censorius,-a,-um of the censors
charta,-ae f., papyrus/made from papyrus
circiter adv., about/nearly/almost
citratus,-a,-um treated with citron- wood oil
colligo,colligere,collegi,collectum to be reckoned (usually in the pass.)
comburo,-buere,-bussi,-bustus to consume/burn up
commentaria,-orum n. pl., memoir/journal
computresco,- putrescere,-putrui to rot
consulatus,-us m., consulship
convenit impers., it is agreed
Cornelius Gnaeus Terentius m., proper noun, the Roman clerk that uncovered a chest of ancient books while plowing his farm
cremo (1) to burn
decretum,-i n., decree
decumus = decimus (tenth)
duro (1) to last/endure/survive
effodio,-fodere,-fodi,-fossum to dig up
etiamnum adv., still/even
exemplum,-i n., example
Gaius Sempronius Tuditanus m., consul in 129 B.C.; wrote the *Libri Magistratum* and a historical work evidenced through fragments
Ianiculum,-i n., the Janiculum Hill
infodio,-fodere,-fodi,-fossum to bury
ingens,ingentis huge/vast
insuper adv., above/on top of
lapis,lapidis m., stone
Marcus Baebius Tamphilus m., consul in 181 B.C.E.
Marcus Varro m., author and polymath
medius,-a,-um situated at the center/in the middle
miraculum,-i n., wonder
namque conj., for/for in fact
Numa Pompilius m., the second king of Rome
Piso Caesoninus m., Piso was appointed censor in 50 B.C. through Julius Caesar's influence
placet, placere, placuit (with acc. + inf.) 3rd impers., it is resolved
pono,ponere,posui,positus to cite
pontificalis,-e pontifical/priestly
pontificius,-a,-um pontifical/priestly
praeceptum,-i n., doctrine/teaching
praetor,praetoris m., praetor, a judicial magistrate in the early Roman Republic
prodo,prodere,prodidi,proditum to transmit/hand down
propterea for that reason/on that account/therefore
Publius Cornelius Cethegus m., consul in 181 B.C.
Pythagoricus,-a,-um Pythagorean/pertaining to the philosopher Pythagoras
quadratus,-a,-um square
quapropter adv., on which account
quia conj., because
quoquoversus adv., in every direction
regnum,-i n., rule/reign
repastino (1) to plow
reddo,reddere,reddidi,redditum to give/render
scriba,-ae m., clerk/scribe
Sibylla,-ae f., sibyl of Cumae whom Aeneas consulted and another who was said to have composed the Sibylline Books which were bought by Tarquinius
sino,sinere,sivi,situm to bury
Spurinus Quintus Petilius m., the praetor urbanus in 181 B.C., who read the philosophy books and, according to Livy, said that he was prepared to give his oath to the Senate (to whom the case had been referred) that the books were subversive of Roman religion and should be burned. The Senate voted that it seemed sufficient that the praetor promised this oath, and the books were burned in the comitium (the open public space in front of the Senate House) in sight of the people.
Tarquinus Superbus m., the seventh and last king of Rome
tango,tangere,tetigi,tactus to touch (i.e., eat holes in)
tinea,-ae f., moth
totidem adv., just as many
vero conj., but
vetustus,-a,-um old
vincio,vincire,vinxi,vinctum to bind/tie around

History of Gardening

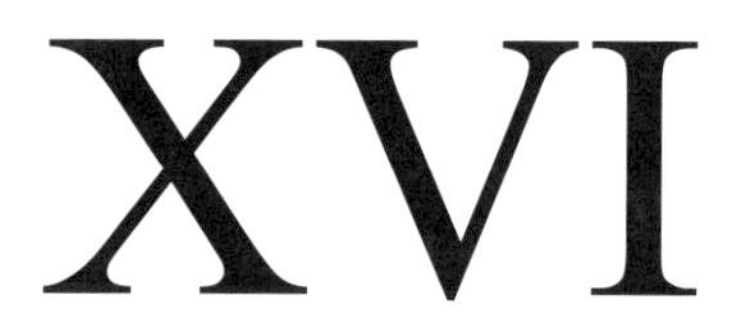

Grammar Review

Jussive Subjunctive	p. 138
Passive Periphrastic	
Subjunctive Indirect Questions	p. 139

New Grammar

-pte is an emphatic particle in old Latin, added to possessive adjectives in the ablative case, e.g., *sua**pte*** = *sua*

Adjectives derived from nouns: ***-inus*** can be appended to the names of plants (or other materials), e.g., *lactuca,-ae* = f., lettuce; *lactuc**inus**,-a,-um* = belonging to lettuce. In this reading, Pliny refers to a branch of the Valerian gens that took on the cognomen of *Lactucinus*, probably as a result of a business interest.

A subordinate clause takes the subjunctive when it expresses the thought of some person other than the speaker or writer.

> . . . *et sic statim faciebant iudicium, nequam esse in domo matrem familias—etenim haec cura feminae dicebatur—**ubi indiligens esset extra hortus:***

> . . . and thus immediately they made a judgment, there was a worthless mistress of the family, and indeed this responsibility was said to be for a woman—**when there was outside a neglected garden**:

A relative clause with the subjunctive is often used to indicate a characteristic of the antecedent.

> *Nec caules ut nunc maxime probabant, damnantes pulmentaria **quae egerent alio pulmentario**.*

> Nor they especially approved vegetables as now, condemning (vegetable) flavors **which had need for another flavor (seasoning)**.

Potential subjunctive expressing a possibility is translated "may."

*Aliqua gratia **contingat** nostrae operae curaeque.*

Some gratitude **may befall** our labor and carefulness.

NB:		
	ago,agere,egi,actum + dat.	to require
	aliqui,aliqua,aliquod	indef. adj., some
	cura,-ae	f., responsibility/careful attention/research
	facere iudicium	to pass judgment (on a person's actions)
	iam	adv., to this time/furthermore
	id erat + inf.	that was (the reason) to ____
	in + acc.	prep., for (the purpose of)
	signum,-i	n., statue
	sive . . . sive	whether . . . or

Sentences

1. Superest reverti ab his herbis ad curam hortorum et natura suapte memorandam quoniam antiquitas mirata est nihil magis quam hortos Hesperidum ac regum Adonidis et Alcinoi, itemque pensiles hortos.

2. Quidem Romani reges ipsi coluere hortos, quippe etiam Tarquinius Superbus suo filio illum saevum atque sanguinarium nuntium ex horto remisit.*

3. Nusquam in XII tabulis est verbum villa in ea significatione; semper nominabatur hortus in ea significatione et horti vero fuerunt in heredium, ob quam rem religio quaedam comitata est.

4. In horto et foro tantum videmus saturica signa dicari in remedio contra effascinationes invidentium, quamquam Plautus hortos tutelae Veneris adsignat.

5. Nunc in urbe ipsa possident delicias villas agrosque. Epicurus, magister otii, Athenis primus instituit hoc; ante eum non fuerat moris rura in oppidis habitari.

6. Prisci agricolas aestumabant ex hortis eorum. Cura horti dicebatur feminae et nequam mater familias in domo fuit, ubi extra hortus indiligens esset.

7. Ea horti maxime placebant quae non egerent igni parcerentque ligno.

8. Pars hortorum pertinens ad condimenta fatetur domi versuram fieri solitam esse, atque non Indicum piper quaesitum neque res quae nunc trans maria petimus.

*According to Livy, Tarquinius cut off the heads of the tallest poppies in his garden as an allegory to instruct his son Sextus Tarquinius to pacify a recently conquered enemy city by executing its leading citizens. This leads to the modern expression "tall poppy syndrome" to describe the phenomenon of tearing down individuals who rise too far above the majority.

9. Iam plebs urbana imagine oculis cotidiana hortorum rura in fenestris suis praebebant, antequam latrocinatio saeva coegit omnes prospectus praefigi.

10. Cognitum est in Valeria familia non puduisse Lactucinos appellari, et aliqua gratia contingat nostrae operae curaeque Vergilio quoque confesso quam difficile sit honorem verborum rebus tam parvis perhibere.

CHAPTER XVI

Translation

Ab his (herbis) superest reverti ad hortorum curam, et suapte natura memorandam et quoniam antiquitas nihil prius mirata est quam Hesperidum hortos ac regum Adonidis et Alcinoi, itemque pensiles, sive illos Semiramis sive Assyriae rex Syrus fecit . . . Romani quidem reges ipsi coluere; quippe etiam Superbus nuntium illum saevum atque sanguinarium filio remisit ex 5 horto. In XII tabulis legum nostrarum nusquam nominatur villa, semper in significatione ea hortus, in horti vero heredium; quam ob rem comitata est et religio quaedam, hortoque et foro tantum contra invidentium effascinationes dicari videmus in remedio saturica signa, quamquam hortos tutelae Veneris adsignante Plauto. Iam quidem hortorum nomine in ipsa urbe delicias agros 10 villasque possident. Primus hoc instituit Athenis Epicurus otii magister; usque ad eum moris non fuerat in oppidis habitari rura.

Hortorum Cato praedicat caules: hinc primum agricolas aestumabant prisci, et sic statim faciebant iudicium, nequam esse in domo matrem familias—etenim haec cura feminae dicebatur—ubi indiligens esset extra 15 hortus . . . Nec caules ut nunc maxime probabant, damnantes pulmentaria quae egerent alio pulmentario: id erat oleo parcere, nam gari desideria etiam in exprobratione erant. Horti maxime placebant quae non egerent igni parcerentque ligno, expedita res et parata semper, unde et acetaria appellantur, facilia concoqui nec oneratura sensus cibo, et quae minime accenderent 20 desiderium. Pars eorum ad condimenta pertinens fatetur domi versuram fieri solitam, atque non Indicum piper quaesitum quaeque trans maria petimus. Iam in fenestris suis plebs urbana imagine hortorum cotidiana oculis rura praebebant, antequam praefigi prospectus omnes coegit multitudinis innumerae saeva latrocinatio. Quamobrem sit aliquis et his honos, neve 25 auctoritatem rebus vilitas adimat, cum praesertim etiam cognomina procerum inde nata videamus, Lactucinosque in Valeria familia non puduisse appellari, et contingat aliqua gratia operae curaeque nostrae Vergilio quoque confesso quam sit difficile verborum honorem tam parvis perhibere.

Vocabulary

accendo,-cendere,-cendi,-cessum to kindle/excite
acetaria,-orum (from *acetum*, vinegar) n. pl., salad
adimo,-imere,-emi,-emptum to deny/take away
Adonis,-idis m., annually renewed, ever-youthful vegetation god, a life-death-rebirth deity whose nature is tied to the calendar. His cult belonged to women.
adsigno (1) to assign/allot
aestumo (1) to estimate/assess
ager,agri m., land in cultivation/farm
Alcinous,-i m., king of Phaecia, possessor of fine orchards
antequam adv., before
antiquitas,-atis f., antiquity
Assyria,-ae f., Assyria, part of Mesopotamia
auctoritas,auctoritatis m., respect/prestige
caulis,-is m., vegetable, esp. cabbage
Cato,-onis m., Cato the Elder, 234–149 B.C. Cato was a conservative politician whose army career took him all over the Roman Empire. While in Carthage he came across Mago's book on agriculture. He combined this information with his own experiences of farming to write *De Re Rustica* (On Agriculture).
cibus,-i m., food
cognomen,-inis n., name
cogo,cogere,coegi,coactum to compel
colo,colere,colui,cultum to cultivate
comitor,comitari to attach to
concoquo,-coquere,-coxi,-coctum to digest
condimentum,-i n., seasoning/condiment
confiteor,-fiteri,-fessus sum to confess
contingo,-tingere,-tigi,-tactum + dat. to befall
cotidianus,-a,-um common/everyday
cura,-ae f., responsibility/careful attention/research
damno (1) to condemn
deliciae,-arum f. pl., luxurious/extravagant conditions or surroundings
desiderium,-i n., desire
dico (1) to dedicate to the gods
effascinatio,-onis f., sorcery
egeo,egere,egui + abl. to be in need of
Epicurus,-i m., the Greek philosopher
etenim conj., and indeed
expeditus,-a,-um expedient/quick
exprobratio,-onis f., reproach
extra adv., outside
fateor,fateri,fassus sum to show/reveal
fenestra,-ae f., window
forum,-i n., the Forum in Rome
garum,-i n., fish sauce
gratia,-ae f., gratitude
habito (1) to dwell in/inhabit
herba,-ae f., plant
heredium,-i n., hereditary estate/patrimony/inheritance
Hesperides,-um f. pl., guardians of the golden apples
hinc adv., henceforth/from this cause/for this reason
honos,honoris m., honor/respect/reverence
hortus,-i m., garden

imago,imaginis f., display
in + acc. for (the purpose of)
inde adv., thence
Indicus,-a,-um Indian
indiligens,-ntis neglected
innumerus,-a,-um countless/innumerable
instituo,instituere,institui,institutum to institute/establish
invidens,-videntis envious
item adv., likewise/also
lactucinus,-a,-um belonging to/related to lettuce
latrocinatio,-onis f., robbery
lignum,-i n., wood
magister,-tri m., connoisseur/master
mater familias,matris familias f., mistress of the family
memoro (1) to talk about/discuss
multitudo,-inis f., multitude
natus,-a,-um derived
nequam indecl. adj., worthless
neve adv., nor
nomino (1) to name/call
nuntium,-i n., message
nusquam adv., nowhere
oleum,-i n., olive oil
onero (1) to burden
opera,-ae f., service/labor
oppidum,-i n., town
paratus,-a,-um available
pars,partis f., a portion
parvus,-a,-um small/lowly
pensilis,-e hanging
perhibeo,-ere,-hibui,-hibitum to bestow/give
pertineo,-tinere,-tinui + ad to pertain to/apply to
piper,piperis n., pepper
placeo,placere,placui,placitum to be approved of/acceptable
Plautus,-i m., T. Maccius Plautus, the Roman comic poet
plebs,plebis f., common people/lower class
possideo,possidere,possedi,possessum to possess/own
praebeo,praebere,praebui,praebitum to provide/give/display
praedico (1) to praise
praefigo,-figere,-fixi,-fixum to close/wall/bar
praesertim adv., especially
primum adv., first of all/above all
priscus,-a,-um ancient/old
prius adv., before
probo (1) to approve
proceres,-um m. pl., nobles, an artificial aristocracy invented by the plebs; title granted to a man and his descendants once the consulship had been achieved
prospectus,-us m., view/sight
pudeo,pudere,pudui,puditum to make ashamed/cause shame
pulmentarium,-i n., flavoring/seasoning (considered an extravagant luxury)
quamobrem (quam ob rem) wherefore/for which reason
quamquam adv., yet
quaesitus,-a,-um to seek
quippe etiam certainly/to be sure
religio,-onis f., sanctity
remitto,-mittere,-misi,-missum to send back
revertor,reverti,reversus sum to return
rus,ruris n., country dwelling/country estate/rural (quality)
sanguinarius,-a,-um bloody
saevus,-a,-um ferocious
saturicus,-a,-um resembling a satyr/satyr-like
Semiramis,-idis f., the king said to have built Babylon
significatio,-onis f., meaning/sense
signum,-i n., statue
solitus,-a,-um accustomed/customary/normal
statim adv., immediately
supersum,-esse,-fui to remain; **superest** 3rd impers., it remains
Syrus,-i m., Cyrus, founder of the Achaemenid dynasty of Persia
tabulae,-arum f. pl., the Twelve Tables, the first Roman Law Code, set up in the Forum as permanent record
tam adv., to such a degree
tantum adv., only
Tarquinius Superbus m., the last king of Rome
tutela,-ae f., guardianship
urbanus,-a,-um urban/of the city
usque adv., all the way to/until
Valerius,-a,-um name of a famous Roman noble family
Venus,-eris f., goddess of love and generation
Vergilius,-i m., Vergil (Publius Vergilius Maro, 70–19 B.C.), the foremost Roman poet of his day. Born in Mantua, he wrote, among other works, the *Georgics* (On Farming). This didactic poem in four books was frequently cited by other classical writers, though more for its literary accomplishment than for its use as a farming manual.
vero adv., in fact
versura,-ae f., borrowing
villa,-ae f., estate
vilitas,-atis f., lowliness

History of Medicine

Grammar Review

Ablative of Separation	p. 150
Gerunds	p. 131
Subjunctive Conditional Statements	p. 139
Subjunctive Purpose Clauses	p. 138

New Grammar

-met is an enclitic particle, attached for emphasis to a pronoun: ***semet*** = *se*

The pronominal adjective, i.e., a word that is primarily a pronoun but sometimes can function as an adjective, *aliquis,aliquid* (someone/something) has an alternate dative and ablative plural form.

	m. pl.	f. pl.	n. pl.
Nom.	*aliqui*	*aliquae*	*aliquae*
Gen.	*aliquorum*	*aliquarum*	*aliquorum*
Dat.	*aliquibus/**aliquis***	*aliquibus/**aliquis***	*aliquibus/**aliquis***
Acc.	*aliquos*	*aliquas*	*aliquae*
Abl.	*aliquibus/**aliquis***	*aliquibus/**aliquis***	*aliquibus/**aliquis***

Perfect active forms for verbs with a perfect active stem ending in *–vi* often appear in shortened forms: *no**sse**t* = *novi**sse**t*

Special subjunctive relative clause of characteristic introduced by *quod*:

> *Antea condiderat Valgius solus apud nos, **quod equidem inveniam**, Pompeius Lenaeus Magni libertus, quo primum tempore hanc scientiam ad nostros pervenisse animo adverto.*
>
> Before Valgius had written, the only man among us, **indeed that I discover**, (was) Pompeius Lenaeus, the freedman of (Pompeius) Magnus, at which time I perceive this knowledge first reached/came to our (people).

Dative of agent is used regularly with gerundives in passive periphrastic constructions, but occasionally it is used with the perfect passive participle:

> ***Uni ei*** *excogitatum.* — **By this one** it was thought out.
> ***(Uni ei) primo*** *inventa genera antidoti.*
> **By this one first** types of an antidote discovered.

Ablatives of respect occur without a preposition and denote in repect to what something is or is done.

> *Asclepiades erat clarus* ***arte*** *medendi.*
>
> Asclepiades was famous **in respect to the art** of healing.

Causal clauses introduced by the conjunction *quoniam* (since) take the indicative when the reason is that of the writer and take the subjunctive when the reason is that of another.

> *(Erat) illius inventum sanguinem anatum Ponticarum miscere antidotis,* ***quoniam veneno viverent****.*
>
> (It was) the discovery of that one to mix the blood of Pontic ducks to antidotes, **since (according to some) they lived by means of poison**.

NB:

ago,agere,egi,actum		to practice (medicine)
animo + adverto,-vertere, -versi,-versum		to perceive/notice
appello (1)		to address
cura,-ae		f., research
doceo,docere,docui,doctum		to point out
facio,facere,feci,factum		to appoint
in + acc.		among
in primis		especially
maxume	=	*maxime*
non alio modo quam		not in another way than/not otherwise than
quā		adv., by what way?/how?
quod		adv., insofar as/that
ratio,rationis		f., method
res,rei		f., benefit
unusquisque	=	*unus quisque* (each one)
virtus,-utis		f., worth

Sentences

Origines Medicinae Romanae

1. Maiores nostri qui erant omnium utilitatium virtutumque rapacissimi minus quam erat par medicinam celebraverunt. M. Cato, omnium bonarum artium magister, primusque et diu solus qui attigit medicinam.
2. Post Catonem solus Gaius Valgius nostrorum virorum inlustrium temptavit scribere de medicina; ante Valgium solus Pompeius Lenaeus libertus Pompeii Magni.
3. Mithridates quem Pompeius Magnus debellavit intellegitur fama argumentisque fuisse praeterquam omnes suos genitores diligentissimum vitae et cotidie venenum bibisse, remediis praesumptis ut consuetudine ipsa venenum innoxium fieret.
4. Unum antidotum etiam nomen eius retinet; erat illius inventum sanguinem anatum Ponticarum miscere antidotis, quoniam veneno viverent.
5. Mithridates de medicina peculiariter curiosus erat et ab omnibus subiectis singula exquisivit; scrinium commentationum harum, et exemplaria effectusque in arcanis rebus suis reliquit. Ad Mithridatem Asclepiades clarus arte medendi misit pro se volumina.
6. Pompeius libertum suum Lenaeum transferre eas commentationes nostro sermone iussit, vitaeque ita illa victoria non minus quam reipublicae profuit.

Medicina Herbarum

7. Homerus gloriam herbarum Aegypto tribuit; narrat Aegyptias herbas a uxore regis traditas esse Helenae suae, ac nobile illud nepenthes adferens oblivionem tristitiae veniamque ab Helena omnibus mortalibus propinandum.
8. Fuit quidem quondam ambitus adoptandi eas herbas nominibus suis. Tanta res videbatur herbam invenire et vitam iuvare nunc fortassis aliquis existimaturis curam hanc nostram esse frivolam quoque.
9. Experimenta aevi iudicaverunt asperrimi cruciatus esse calculorum a stillicidio vesicae, proximum stomachi, tertium eorum quae in capite doleant, non ob alios morbos fere morte conscita.
10. Miror noxias herbas esse demonstratas a Graecis, non venenorum tantum, quoniam ea conditio vitae est ut plerumque mori etiam optimis viris portus sit.
11. Ego nec abortiva ac ne amatoria quidem dico. Satis operae fuerit dixisse herbas salutares vitae.

Antiqua Medicina et Asclepiades

12. Asclepiades erat aetate Magni Pompei orandi magister sed non satis in arte ea quaestuosus; ut erat vir sagacis ingenii ad alia quam forum, se repente ad medicinam convertit.

13. Cum non egisset medicinam nec remedia percipienda oculis usuque nosset, omnia abdicavit totamque medicinam ad causas revocando coniecturae fecit.

14. Asclepiades professus est quinque res maxume communium auxiliorum: abstinentiam cibi, alias vini, fricationem corporis, ambulationem, gestationes.

Translation

Origines Medicinae Romanae

Minus hoc quam par erat nostri celebravere omnium utilitatium et virtutum rapacissimi, primusque et diu solus idem ille M. Cato, omnium bonarum artium magister, paucis (verbis) dumtaxat attigit. . . . Post eum unus inlustrium temptavit Gaius Valgius. . . .

Antea condiderat solus apud nos, quod equidem inveniam, Pompeius Lenaeus Magni libertus, quo primum tempore hanc scientiam ad nostros pervenisse animo adverto. Namque Mithridates, maximus sua aetate regum quem debellavit Pompeius, omnium ante se genitorum diligentissimus vitae fuisse argumentis praeterquam fama intellegitur. Uni ei excogitatum cotidie venenum bibere praesumptis remediis ut consuetudine ipsa innoxium fieret; primo inventa genera antidoti ex quibus unum etiam nomen eius retinet; illius inventum sanguinem anatum Ponticarum miscere antidotis, quoniam veneno viverent; ad illum Asclepiadis medendi arte clari volumina composita extant, cum sollicitatus ex urbe Roma praecepta pro se mitteret; illum solum mortalium certum est XXII linguis locutum, nec e subiectis gentibus ullum hominem per interpretem appellatum ab eo annis LVI quibus regnavit. Is ergo in reliqua ingenii magnitudine medicinae peculiariter curiosus et ab omnibus subiectis, qui fuere magna pars terrarum, singula exquirens scrinium commentationum harum et exemplaria effectusque in arcanis suis reliquit, Pompeius autem omni praeda regia potitus transferre ea sermone nostro

5 10 15 20

libertum suum Lenaeum grammaticae artis iussit, vitaeque ita profuit non minus quam reipublicae victoria illa.

Medicina Herbarum

. . . Neque aliud mirata magis antiquitas reperietur. . . . Homerus quidem primus doctrinarum et antiquitatis parens, multus alias in admiratione Circae, gloriam herbarum Aegypto tribuit. . . . Herbas certe Aegyptias a regis uxore traditas Helenae suae plurimas narrat ac nobile illud nepenthes oblivionem tristitiae veniamque adferens et ab Helena utique omnibus mortalibus propinandum. 25

Fuit quidem et hic quondam ambitus nominibus suis eas adoptandi, ut docebimus fecisse reges. Tanta res videbatur herbam invenire, vitam iuvare, nunc fortassis aliquis curam hanc nostram frivolam quoque existimaturis; adeo deliciis sordent etiam quae ad salutem pertinent. Auctores tamen quarum inveniuntur in primis celebrari par est effectu earum digesto in genera morborum. Qua quidem in reputatione misereri sortis humanae subit, praeter fortuita casusque et quae nova omnis hora excogitat, milia morborum singulis mortalium timenda. Qui gravissimi ex his sint discernere stultitiae prope videri possit, cum suus cuique ac praesens quisque atrocissimus videatur. Et de hoc tamen iudicavere aevi experimenta, asperrimi cruciatus esse calculorum a stillicidio vesicae, proximum stomachi, tertium eorum quae in capite doleant, non ob alios fere morte conscita. 30 35 40

A Graecis et noxias herbas demonstratas miror equidem, nec
venenorum tantum, quoniam ea conditio vitae est ut mori plerumque etiam
optimis portus sit, tradatque M. Varro Servium Clodium equitem Romanum
magnitudine doloris in podagra coactum veneno crura perunxisse et postea 45
caruisse sensu omni aeque quam dolore in ea parte corporis. Sed quae fuit
venia monstrandi qua mentes solverentur, partus eliderentur, multaque
similia? Ego nec abortiva dico ac ne amatoria quidem, nec alia magica
portenta, nisi ubi cavenda sunt aut coarguenda. . . . Satis operae fuerit
abundeque praestatum, vitae salutares dixisse ac pro ea inventas. 50

Antiqua Medicina et Asclepiades

Durabat tamen antiquitas firma magnasque confessae rei vindicabat
reliquias, donec Asclepiades aetate Magni Pompei orandi magister nec
satis in arte ea quaestuosus, ut ad alia quam forum sagacis ingenii, huc se
repente convertit atque, ut necesse erat homini qui nec id egisset nec
remedia nosset oculis usuque percipienda, torrenti ac meditata cotidie 55
oratione blandiens omnia abdicavit totamque medicinam ad causas
revocando coniecturae fecit, quinque res maxume communium auxiliorum
professus, abstinentiam cibi, alias vini, fricationem corporis, ambulationem,
gestationes, quae cum unusquisque semet ipsum sibi praestare posse
intellegeret, faventibus cunctis velut essent vera quae facillima erant, 60
universum prope humanum genus circumegit in se non alio modo quam si
caelo demissus advenisset.

Vocabulary

abdico (1) to reject/renounce
abortivus,-a,-um abortive
abstinentia,-ae f., abstention
abunde adv., abundantly/amply
adeo adv., to such an extent
adfero,adferre,attuli,allatum to bring
admirato,-onis f., admiratrion
adopto (1) to adopt
advenio,-venire,-veni,-ventum to come
Aegyptius,-a,-um Egyptian
Aegyptus,-i f., Egypt
aeque adv., equally
aevum,-i n., time
alias adv., at another time/elsewhere
amatorium,-i n., a love potion
ambitus,-us m., ambition
ambulatio,-onis f., walking
anas,anatis f., duck
animo + adverto,-vertere,-versi,-versum to perceive/notice
antea adv., before then
antidotum,-i n., antidote
antiquitas,-atis f., antiquity
appello (1) to address
arcanus,-a,-um private
argumentum,-i n., evidence/proof
Asclepiades,-is m., a teacher of rhetoric who later practiced medicine in Rome; died about 40 B.C.
asper,-era,-erum severe/sharp
atrox,-ocis adj., atrocious/awful
attingo,-tingere,-tigi,-tactum to mention
auctor,auctoris m., author/discoverer (of a piece of information)
auditio,-onis f., listening/hearing
bibo,bibere,bibi,bibitum to drink
blandior,blandiri,blanditus sum to flatter/charm
calculus,-i m., stone
capito,-onis m., head
casus,-us m., mishap/accident
caveo,cavere,cavi,cautum to guard against
celebro (1) to praise
cibus,-i m., food
Circe,-ae f., Circe, an enchantress/witch
circumago,-agere,-egi,-actum to bring around (views/opinions)
coarguo,-arguere,-argui to prove to be wrong/denounce
cogo,cogere,coegi,coactum to compel
commentatio,-onis f., study/written description/notebook
compositus,-a,-um composed/addressed
conditio,-onis f., condition/state
condo,condere,condidi,conditum to write
confiteor,-fiteri,-fessus sum to acknowledge
coniectura,-ae f., guesswork/conjecture
conscisco,-sciscere,-scivi,-scitum to resolve/inflict upon oneself
consuetudo,-inis f., custom/habit
converto,-vertere,-verti,-versum to change/convert
cotidie adv., daily
cruciatus,-us m., pain/torture/agony
crus,cruris n., leg
cunctus,-a,-um all
curiosus,-a,-um + gen. curious about
damno (1) to condemn
debello (1) to conquer
defetus,-us m., eclipse
deliciae,-arum f. pl., extravagant tastes/extravagant notions
demittto,-mittere,-misi,-missum to send down
demonstro (1) to describe
digero,-gerere,-gessi,-gestum to arrange
diligens,diligentis attentive
discerno,-cernere,-crevi,-cretum to distinguish/discern
divus,-a,-um deified
do,dare,dedi,datum to give/hand over
doceo,docere,docui,doctum to point out
doctrina,-ae f., teaching/learning
doleo,dolere,dolui,doliturus to cause pain
dolor,-oris m., pain
donec conj., until
dumtaxat adv., not more than/at most
duro (1) to continue/endure
effectus,-us m., effects/property
elido,-lidere,-lisi,-lisum to abort/expel
equites,-um m. pl., a social order in the Roman state ranked between the patricians and the plebs
equidem adv., indeed
ergo as I was saying
excogito (1) to think out/devise
existimo (1) to judge/evaluate
experimentum,-i n., experience
exquiro,-quirere,-quisivi,-quisitum to search out
exto,extare,extiti to exist
facio,facere,faci,factum to appoint/relegate
fama,-ae f., rumor/report
faveo,favere,favi,fatum to favor/support
fere adv., generally/as a rule

firmus,-a,-um strong/steadfast
forum,-i n., court of law
fortassis adv., perhaps
fortuitus,-a,-um chance/accidental
fricatio,-onis f., massage
frivolus,-a,-um frivolous/worthless
Gaius Valgius m., an Augustan poet and grammarian
genitor,-oris m., ancestor
gestatio,-onis f., carriage ride
gloria,-ae f., renown
grammaticus,-a,-um literary/grammatical
gratus,-a,-um pleasing
herba,-ae f., herb/plant
huc adv., to this
imperator,-oris m., general
indico (1) to make known/show
ingenium,-i n., ability/genius
inlustris,-e distinguished
innoxius,-a,-um harmless
interpres,-etis m/f, interpreter
inveho,-vehere,-vexi,-vectum to bring in/carry in
inventum,-i n., discovery
Italus,-a,-um Italian
iudico (1) to decide/judge
libertus,-i m., a freedman
lingua,-ae f., language
Lucius Lucullus m., famous Roman general
magicus,-ae,-um magical
magnitudo,-inis f., magnitude/greatness
maiores,-um m. pl., ancestors
Marcus Porcius Cato, m., the supporter of Pompey who committed suicide after being defeated in Africa by armies loyal to Julius Caesar
Marcus Varro m., the polymath Marcus Terentius Varro, 116–27 B.C.
medeor,mederi + dat. to heal/cure
medicina,-ae f., medicine/practice of medicine
meditatus,-a,-um prepared/meditated
memor,-oris adj., remembering/mindful
miror,mirari,miratus sum to marvel at/be astonished by
misceo,miscere,miscui,mixtum to mix in/to introduce as an ingredient
misereor,misereri + gen. to pity/have compassion for
Mithridates,-is m., Mithridates VI, king of Pontus, fought Rome in three wars and was defeated by Sulla, Lucullus, and Pompey
monstro (1) to point out/show
morbus,-i m., disease
namque conj., for/for even/for in fact
nepenthes,-is n., a drug supposed to remove all sorrow
nobilis,-is,-e renowned/famous
nosco,noscere,novi,notum to learn/become acquainted with
novo (1) brought into existence
noxius,-a,-um harmful
oblivio,-onis f., forgetfulness
omitto,omittere,omisi,omissum to omit/leave out
opera,-ae f., service
oratio,-onis f., oration
oro (1) to speak before a court/plead a case
parens,-ntis m., parent
pars,paris appropriate/deserved/right
partus,-us m., fetus
paulitim adv., little by little
percipio,-cipere,-cepi,-ceptum to acquire
peculiariter adv., especially
pertineo,-tinere,-tinui to pertain
perungo,-ungere,-unxi,-unctum to smear/rub with ointment
pervenio,-venire,-veni,-ventum to reach/come to
plerumque adv., very often
podagra,-ae f., gout
Pompeius Lenaeus m., the freedman of Pompey the Great
Pompeius Magnus m., Pompey the Great
Ponticus,-a,-um of the Black Sea
portentum,-i n., portent
portus,-us m., refuge
postea adv., afterward
potior,potiri,potitus sum + abl. to obtain/seize
praeceptum,-i n., instruction
praeda,-ae f., booty
praesens,-ntis (partic. of *praesum)* present at the moment
praesto,-stare,-stiti,-statum to provide
praesumo,-sumere,-sumpsi,-sumptum to take beforehand
praeter adv., besides
praeterquam adv., more than/beyond
primum adv., for the first time/first
proficiscor,-ficisci,profectus sum to avow/enumerate
profiteor,-fiteri,-fessus sum to avow/declare
prope adv., almost
propino (1) to give (drink)/administer
prosum,prodesse,profui + dat. to be beneficial
proximum adv., next
quaestuosus,-a,-um rich/profitable
quisque,quidque pronoun/adj., each/every
quoque adv., too/even
rapax,-acis rapacious/avaricious
ratio,rationis f., method

regius,-a,-um royal
regno (1) to reign
reliquiae,-arum f. pl., remnants/remains
reliquus,-a,-um other than already specified
repente adv., suddenly
repo,repere,repsi,reptum to crawl
reputatio,-onis f., reflection/consideration
retineo,-tinere,-tinui,-tentum to keep/retain
revoco (1) to refer to/apply to/resort to
sagax,-acis adj., keen/acute
salus,-utis f., physical well-being/health
salutaris,-e healthy/wholesome
sanguen,-inis n., blood
scrinium,-i n., a case/box
sensus,-us m., sensation
sermo,-onis m., language/dialect
Servius Clodius m., a Roman knight
singulus,-a,-um unique/remarkable/individual
sollicito (1) to solicit/repeatedly seek
solveo,solvere,solvi,solutum to weaken/impair
sordeo,-ere to appear worthless/seem worthless
sors,sortis f., lot
stillicidium,-i n., a blockage (to the flow of urine from the bladder)
stomachus,-i m., stomach
stultitia,-ae f., foolishness/folly
subeo,-ire,-ii,-itum to come into the mind
subiectus,-i m., subject
tantum adv., only
tempto (1) to try/attempt
torrens,-ntis adj., torrential
trado,tradere,tradidi,traditum to hand down/ establish
transfero,-ferre,-tuli,-latum to translate
tribuo,tribuere,tribui,tributum to ascribe
tristitia,-ae f., unhappiness
universus,-a,-um all
unusquisque (unus quisque) each one
usus,-us m., practical experience
utilitas,-atis f., useful thing
utique adv., without condition/qualification
uxor,-oris f., spouse
velut adv., just as/in the same way that
virtus,virtutis f., worth (gen. case)
venia,-ae f., excuse/justification/pardon
venenum,-i n., poison
vesica,-ae f., bladder
victoria,-ae f., victory
vindico (1) to lay claim to/appropriate
virtus,-utis f., worth
volumen,-inis n., book

Remedies Depending on the Will

Grammar Review

Ablative of Separation	p. 150
Gerundive of Purpose	
Gerunds	p. 131
Subjunctive Conditional Statements	p. 139

New Grammar

quis/quid can be used as indefinite pronouns, in which case their translation is "any."
quid eorum = any of these things

NB:	*ab*	prep., on
	alias . . . alias	sometimes . . . sometimes
	animus,-i	m., will/resolve
	in + abl.	in/among
	in + acc.	on
	in primis	especially
	plurimum	supl. adv., most often

Translation

. . . Abstinere cibo omni aut potu, alias vino tantum aut carne, alias balneis, cum quid eorum postulet valetudo, in praesentissimis remediis habetur. His adnumeratur excercitatio, intentio vocis, ungui, fricari cum ratione. Vehemens enim fricatio spissat, lenis mollit, multa adimit corpus, auget modica. In primis vero prodest ambulatio, gestatio et ea pluribus modis, equitatio 5 stomacho et coxis utilissima, phthisi navigatio, longis morbis locorum mutatio, item somno sibi mederi aut lectulo aut rara vomitione. Supini cubitus oculis conducunt, at proni tussibus, in latera adversum destillationes. Aristoteles et Fabianus plurimum somniari circa ver et autumnum tradunt, magisque supino cubitu, at prono nihil, Theophrastus celerius concoqui 10 dextri lateris incubitu, difficilius a supinis. Sol quoque remediorum maximum ab ipso sibi praestari potest, sicuti linteorum strigiliumque vehementia. Perfundere caput calida ante balnearum vaporationem et postea frigida saluberrimum intellegitur, item praesumere et cibis et interponere frigidam eiusdemque potu somnos antecedere et, si libeat, interrumpere. Notandum 15 nullum animal aliud calidos potus sequi ideoque non esse naturales. Mero ante somnos colluere ora propter halitus, frigida matutinis inpari numero ad cavendos dentium dolores, item posca oculos contra lippitudines, certa experimenta sunt, sicut totius corporis valetudinem iuvari varietate victus inobservata. Hippocrates tradit non prandentium celerius senescere exta. 20 Verum id remediis cecinit, non epulis, quippe multo utilissima est temperantia in cibis.

Vocabulary

abstineo,-stinere,-stenui,-stentum to abstain/fast
adimo,-imere,-emi,-emptum to take away/reduce
adnumero (1) to include/count as equal
adversum against (i.e., to guard against)
ambulatio,-onis f., walking
antecedo,-cedere,-cessi,-cessum to precede
Aristoteles,-is m., Aristotle
at conj., but
augeo,augere,auxi,auctum to make grow
autumnus,-i m., autumn
balneae,-arum f. pl., a bath
calida,-ae f., hot water
cano,canere,cecini,cantum to prescribe
carnis,carnis m., meat
caveo,cavere,cavi,cautum to guard against
certus,-a,-um resolved
cibus,-i m., food
circa adv., around
collueo,colluere,collui,collutum to wash/rinse
concoquo,-coquere,-cocoxi,-coctum to digest
conduco,-ducere,-duxi,-ductum to be of use
coxa,-ae f., hip
cubitus,-us m., lying down
dens,dentis m., tooth
destillatio,-onis f., nasal drips
dexter,-tra,-trum on the right/right
epulo,epulonis m., a feaster
epulum ,-i n., a feast
equitatio,-onis f., horseback riding
excercitatio,-onis f., physical exercise
experior,-periri,-pertus sum to prove/know by experience
exta,extorum n. pl., internal organs
Fabianus,-i m., philosopher, teacher of Seneca the Younger
fricatio,-onis f., massage
frico,fricare,fricui,frictum to rub
frigida,-ae f., cold water
gestatio,gestationis f., carriage rides
halitus,-us m., bad breath
Hippocrates,-is m., Hippocrates of Cos (ca. 460 B.C.–ca. 370 B.C.), a Greek physician referred to as the "father of Western medicine" for his lasting contributions as the founder of the Hippocratic school of medicine. This intellectual school revolutionized medicine in ancient Greece and established it as a discipline distinct from those with which it had traditionally been associated (theurgy and philosophy), thus establishing medicine as a profession.
ideo adv., for that reason
incubitus,-us m., lying (down)/reclining
inobservatus,-a,-um casual/haphazard
inpar,inparis uneven
intentio,-onis f., exercising
interpono,-ponere,-posui,-positum to interpose
interrumpo,-rumpere,-rupi,-ruptum to break in the middle
item adv., likewise
latus,lateris n., the side
lectulus,-i m., rest
lenis,-e gentle
libet,libere,libuit,libitum est 3rd impers., to be pleasing/agreeable
linteus,-i m., towel
lippitudo,-inis f., inflammation of the eyes
matutinus,-a,-um in the morning
medicina,-ae f., medicine
medeor,mederi + dat. to heal/help
merum,-i n., wine unmixed with water/neat wine
modicus,-a,-um moderate
mollio,mollire,mollivi,mollitum to make soft
morbus,-i m., disease
mutatio,-onis f., a change
naturales,-e natural
navigatio,-onis f., a sea voyage
noto (1) to mark
os,oris n., mouth
perfundo,-fundere,-fidi,-fusum to bathe/pour over
phthisis,-is f., consumption
posca,poscae f., vinegar
postea adv., afterwards
postulo (1) to demand
potus,-us m., drink/beverage
praesens,-ntis powerful/effective
praesto,-stare,-stiti,-stitum to perform administer/offer
praesumo,-sumere,-sumpsi,-sumptum to take before
prandeo,prandere,prandi, prandium to eat lunch
prodeo,-ire,-ii,-itum to appear
pronus,-a,-um (lying) on the stomach
prosum,prodesse,profui to be of benefit/useful
rarus,-a,-um occasional
ratio,rationis f., method
quippe adv., certainly
saluber,-bris,-bre healthy/salubrious
senesco,senescere,senui to age
sequor,sequi,secutus sum to seek
sicut/sicuti adv., just as

sol,solis m., sun
somnio (1) to dream
somnus,-i m., sleep
spisso (1) to harden
stomachus,-i n., the esophagus
strigilis,-is f., scraper
supinus,-a,-um (lying) on the back
tantum adv., only
temperantia,-ae f., self-control moderation
Theophrastus,-i m., a Greek philosopher
tussis,-is f., cough
unguo,unguere,unxi,unctum to anoint
utilis,-e beneficial
valetudo,-inis f., health
vaporatio,-onis steaming
varietas,-atis f., variety
vehemens,-entis vigorous
vehementia,-ae f., vigorous use
vel adv., even
ver,veris n., spring
vero adv., indeed
verum adv., but
victus,-us m., habit
vomitio,-onis f., vomiting
vox,vocis f., voice

Origin of Magic

New Grammar

1st-declension singular Greek nouns with a genitive ending in ***–ae*** or ***-es*** follow these declension patterns:

Xerxes,-ae = m., Xerxes		*magice,-es f.,* magic/sorcery
Nom.	*Xerxes*	*magice*
Gen.	*Xerx**ae***	*magic**es***
Dat.	*Xerxae*	*magicae*
Acc.	*Xerxen*	*magicen*
Abl.	*Xerxe*	*magice*

NB:

ad + acc.	regarding
apud + acc.	before/with
genus humanum	the human race
hoc	adv., to this (total amount)
in tantum	so entirely
intellego,intellegere, intellexi,intellectum	to recognize
sese =	*se*

Sentences

1. Nemo miretur auctoritatem ei arti maximam fuisse, quando magice sola artium tres alias imperiosissimas humanae mentis complexa in unam se redegit.

2. Nemo dubitabit magicen natam esse primum e medicina ac velut specie salutari inrepsisse altiorem sanctioremque medicinam, ita blandissimis desideratissimisque promissis addidisse vires religionis atque, ut hoc, quoque successerit, miscuisse artes mathematicas.

3. Ita sensibus hominum possessis vinculo triplici in tantum fastigii adolevit magice ut hodie in magna parte gentium praevaleat.

4. Sine dubio magice orta est in Perside a Zoroastre, ut inter auctores convenit. Sed non satis constat an hic Zoroastre fuerit unus solus aut alius postea fuerit.

5. Eudoxus prodidit hunc Zoroastrem fuisse sex milibus annorum ante mortem Platonis, sic ut Aristoteles.

6. Osthanes primus commentatus est quod exstat de ea arte, comitatus Xerxen regem Persarum in bello quod is Graeciae intulit. Ac obiter Osthanes sparsit velut semina portentosae artis, mundo infecto quacumque commeaverant.

Translation

Auctoritatem ei maximam fuisse nemo miretur, quando quidem sola artium tres alias imperiosissimas humanae mentis complexa in unam se redegit. Natam primum e medicina nemo dubitabit ac specie salutari inrepsisse velut altiorem sanctioremque medicinam, ita blandissimis desideratissimisque promissis addidisse vires religionis, ad quas maxime etiamnunc caligat 5 humanum genus, atque, ut hoc, quoque successerit, miscuisse artes mathematicas, nullo non avido futura de sese sciendi atque ea e caelo verissime peti credente. Ita possessis hominum sensibus triplici vinculo in tantum fastigii adolevit ut hodieque etiam in magna parte gentium praevaleat et in oriente regum regibus imperet. 10

Sine dubio illic orta in Perside a Zoroastre, ut inter auctores convenit. Sed unus hic fuerit an postea et alius non satis constat. Eudoxus, qui inter sapientiae sectas clarissimam utilissimamque eam intellegi voluit, Zoroastrem hunc sex milibus annorum ante Platonis mortem fuisse prodidit, sic et Aristoteles. . . . Maxime tamen mirum est in bello Troiano tantum de 15 arte ea silentium fuisse Homero tantumque operis ex eadem in Ulixis erroribus, adeo ut totum opus non aliunde constet . . . Primus, quod exstet, ut equidem invenio, commentatus est de ea Osthanes Xerxen regem Persarum bello quod is Graeciae intulit comitatus, ac velut semina artis portentosae sparsit obiter infecto quacumque commeaverant mundo. . . . 20 Est et alia magices factio a Mose . . . ac Iudeis pendens, multis milibus annorum post Zoroastrem.

Vocabulary

addo,addere,addidi,additum to add
adeo adv., to such an extent
adolesco,adolescere,adolevi in another way
aliunde adv., for a different reason
Aristoteles,-is m., Aristotle
auctoritas,-atis f., support/popularity
avidus,-a,-um eager
blandus,-a,-um seductive
caligo (1) to be in darkness
clarus,-a,-um illustrious
comitatus,-a,-um accompanied
commentor,-ari to write
commeo (1) to travel
complector, complecti, complexus sum to embrace
consto,-stare,-steti,-statum to rest upon/depend/be understood; **constat** 3rd impers., it is agreed
convenit 3rd impers., it is agreed
desideratus,-a,-um welcome/desired
dubium,-i n., doubt
error,erroris m., wandering
etiamnunc even now/yet
Eudoxus,-i m., Eudoxus of Cnidus, 390–340 B.C., famous philosopher, mathematician, astronomer, geographer
exsto,exstare,exstiti to be extant
factio,-onis f., faction
fastigium,-i n., (the period of) intense severity (of a disease)
futurus,-a,-um future
hodie adv., today
Homerus,-i m., the poet Homer
illic adv., there/that place
imperiosissimus,-a,-um most demanding/most domineering
impero (1) to give commands to
infero,inferre,intuli,inlatum to bring in/carry in
inficio,-ficere,-feci,-fectum to infect
inrepo,inrepere,inrepsi to creep in
Iudeus,-a,-um of or belonging to Judaea or its people/Jewish
magice,-es f., magic/sorcery
mathematicus,-a,-um relating to astrology/astrological
medicina,-ae f., medicine
misceo,miscere,miscui,mixtum to mix in/add
Moses,-is m., Moses, the Jewish lawgiver
obiter adv., on the way/in passing
oriens,orientis m., the East
orior,oriri,ortus sum to arise
Osthanes,-is m., a Persian magus who accompanied Xerxes in his invasion of Greece in the early 5th century B.C. Later on, Pliny says, there was a second Osthanes contemporary with and companion of Alexander in the late 4th century B.C. According to Pliny, one of these Osthanes introduced magic to Greece.
pendeo,pendere,pependi to derive/originate from
Perses,-ae m., a Persian
Persis,-idis f., Persia
Plato,Platonis m., Greek philosopher
portentosus,-a,-um monstrous/unnatural
possido,-sidere,-sedi,-sessum to possess/hold
postea adv., afterward
praevaleo,-valere,-valui to prevail/dominate
primum adv., at first
prodo,prodere,prodidi,proditum to transmit/hand down
promissum,-i n., promise/assurance
quacumque adv., by whatever route/way
redigo, redigere,redegi,redactum to convert/bring into/adopt into
religio,-onis f., religion
salutaris,-is curative/promoting health
sanctus,-a,-um holy/sacred
secta,-ae f., philosophical school
semen,seminis n., seed
silentium,-i n., silence
spargo,spargere,sparsi,sparsum to sow/scatter
species,-ei f., pretense/representation
succedo,-cedere,-cessi,-cessum to succeed/advance/move on
superstitio,-onis f., superstition
triplex,-icis triple/threefold
Troianus,-a,-um Trojan
velut adv., as if/just as
vinculum,-i n., tie/bond
utilis,-e useful
utique adv., at least/certainly
Ulixes,-is m., Ulysses, hero of the *Odyssey*
Xerxes,-ae m., king of Persia, 485–465 B.C.
Zoroastres,-is m., Zoroaster, the founder of Magian religion; traditionally dated in the period immediately following Alexander's conquest of the Achaemenid Empire in 330 B.C. The Seleucid kings who gained power after Alexander's death instituted an "Age of Alexander" as the new calendrical epoch. The Zoroastrian priesthood then attempted to establish an "Age of Zoroaster." To do so, they needed to establish when Zoroaster had lived, which they accomplished by counting back the length of successive generations until they concluded that Zoroaster must have lived "258 years before Alexander." This led to speculation that there were two different persons named Zoroaster.

Gold Rings and the Wearing of Rings by the Equestrian Order

Grammar Review

Ablative of Separation	p. 150
eo,ire,ii,itum	p. 132
Locative Case	
ne quis/ne quid	p. 23
Subjunctive Result Clauses	pp. 138, 139

New Grammar

Abbreviations:

C. = Gaius	re. p. = res publica
cos. = consul	HS = sesterces (Roman silver coins)

Duration of time is occasionally expressed in the ablative case:

Longe certe tempore **Certainly for a long time**

Potential subjunctive expresses possibility:

De regibus Romanis non facile ***dixerim***.

Concerning Roman kings not indisputably **I might speak**

Alternate plural forms for *is,ea,id*:

	m.	f.	n.
Nom.	*ei,**ii,i***	*Eae*	*ea*
Gen.	*eorum*	*Earum*	*eorum*
Dat.	*eis,**iis,is***	*eis, **iis,is***	*eis, **iis,is***
Acc.	*eos*	*eas*	*ea*
Abl.	*eis, **iis,is***	*eis, **iis,is***	*eis, **iis,is***

*Siquidem **iis** tantum, qui legati ad exteras gentes ituri essent,*
anuli aurei publice dabantur.

Since only **to those**, who were about to go (as) envoys to foreign nations,
were gold rings publicly given.

Impersonal verbs appear in 3rd-person singular; the subject is translated as "***it***."

constat	**it** is well known	*traditur* **it** is recorded
consitutum est	**it** was agreed	

Seating in Public Places

In 87 B.C. a law assigned to the equites the first 14 rows of seats in theaters. Later on, Augustus passed the *Lex Iulia Theatralis* that established a place for all the classes in such public places as theaters, amphitheaters, and circuses. Of course the senators had the seats nearest to the action, then came the equites, military men, married men, boys and their teachers, noncitizens, plebs, and, last of all, women. These rules were enforced everywhere in the empire.

NB:		
	capio,capere,cepi,captum	to hold/contain
	circa + *acc. acc.*	applying to/concerning
	facio,facere,feci,factum	to commit
	habeo,habere,habui,habitum	to wear
	facile	adv., indisputably
	forma,-ae	f., regulation
	ex + abl.	concerning
	in + acc. acc. (to indicate purpose)	for
	in publico	in public
	utor,uti,usus sum + abl.	to wear
	vice (abl. of *vicis*) + gen.	as a substitute/in place of

Sentences

Origo Anulorum

1. Qui primus induit aurum digitis, pessimum scelus vitae fecit. Nec quis hoc fecerit traditur.
2. Antiquitas voluit intellegi ferreum anulum datum Prometheo vinculum non gestamen.
3. Quis non fateatur historiam etiam fabulosiorem anulo circumacto ut nemo cerneret eum habentem Midae anulum?
4. Manus et prorsus sinistrae maximam auctoritatem auro conciliavere. Non quidem manus Romanae, quarum in more anuli ferrei erant ut virtutis bellicae insigne.
5. De regibus Romanis non facile dixerim. Statua Romuli in Capitolio nullum anulum habet, nec alia statua praeter Numae Serviique Tullii ac ne Lucii quidem Bruti.
6. Hoc in Tarquiniis maxime miror, quorum e Graecia origo fuit, unde hic anulorum usus venit. Sed constat filium donatum esse a suo patre Prisco Tarquinio bulla aurea, cum in praetextae annis occidisset hostem.
7. Unde mos bullae duravit, ut filii eorum, qui equo meruissent, insigne id haberent, ceteri filii lorum haberent, et ideo miror Tarquinii eius statuam sine anulo esse.
8. Longo certe tempore est manifestum ne senatum quidem Romanum anulos aureos habuisse. Siquidem iis tantum, qui legati ad exteras gentes ituri essent, anuli aurei publice dabantur.
9. Neque aliis mos uti fuit quam qui ex ea causa publice anulos accepissent. Ii, qui ob legationem aureos anulos acceperant, in publico tantum iis utebantur, intra domos vero ferreis anulis utebantur, quo argumento etiam nunc sponsae muneris vice ferreus anulus sine gemma mittitur.

Equester Ordo

10. Nono anno principatu Tiberii, equester ordo in unitatem venit, anulorumque auctoritati forma constituta est C. Asinio Pollione et C. Antistio Vetere cos. anno urbis conditae DCCLXXV.
11. Constitutum est, ne cui ius anulorum aureorum esset nisi qui ingenuus ipse, ingenuo patre, avo paterno HS $\overline{\text{CCCC}}$ census fuisset et lege Iulia theatrali qui in quattuordecim ordinibus sedisset.
12. Postea gregatim insigne id coepit adpeti. Quoniam ferreo anulo et iudices equitesque intellegebantur. Adeoque id promiscuum esse coepit, ut in censura Claudii Caesaris, unus ex equitibus, Flavius Proculus, CCCC reos ex ea causa postularet.

13. Gracchi fratres primi omnium instituere separare eum ordinem appellatione iudicum in contumeliam senatus. Mox auctoritas nominis vario seditionum eventu debellata est et appellatio circa publicanos substitit et aliquamdiu tertiae sortis viri publicani fuere.

14. Demum M. Cicero equestre nomen stabilivit Catilinianis rebus et celebravit ex eo ordino profectum esse se. Ab illo tempore, plane, hoc tertium corpus in re publica factum est. Equester ordo senatui populoque Romano coepit adici. Qua de causa nunc post populum scribitur, quia novissime coeptus est adici.

Translation

Origo Anulorum

Pessimum vitae scelus fecit qui primus induit aurum digitis, nec hoc quis fecerit traditur. Nam de Prometheo omnia fabulosa arbitror, quamquam illi quoque ferreum anulum dedit antiquitas vinculumque id, non gestamen, intellegi voluit. Midae quidem anulum, quo circumacto habentem nemo cerneret, quis non etiam fabulosiorem fateatur? Manus et prorsus sinistrae 5 maximam auctoritatem conciliavere auro, non quidem Romanae, quarum in more ferrei erant ut virtutis bellicae insigne.

De regibus Romanis non facile dixerim. Nullum habet Romuli in Capitolio statua nec praeter Numae Serviique Tullii alia ac ne Lucii quidem Bruti. Hoc in Tarquiniis maxime miror, quorum e Graecia fuit origo, unde 10 hic anulorum usus venit, quamquam etiam nunc Lacedaemone ferreo utuntur. Sed a Prisco Tarquinio omnium primo filium, cum in praetextae annis occidisset hostem, bulla aurea donatum constat, unde mos bullae duravit, ut eorum, qui equo meruissent, filii insigne id haberent ceteri lorum; et ideo miror Tarquinii eius statuam sine anulo esse. . . . Longo 15 certe tempore ne senatum quidem Romanum habuisse aureos manifestum est, siquidem iis tantum, qui legati ad exteras gentes ituri essent, anuli publice dabantur, credo, quoniam ita exterorum honoratissimi intellegebantur. Neque aliis uti mos fuit quam qui ex ea causa publice accepissent. . . . Ii quoque, qui ob legationem acceperant aureos, in publico 20 tantum utebantur iis, intra domos vero ferreis, quo argumento etiam nunc sponsae muneris vice ferreus anulus mittitur, isque sine gemma. Equidem nec Iliacis temporibus ullos fuisse anulos video. . . .

Equester Ordo

Tiberii demum principatu nono anno in unitatem venit equester ordo, anulorumque auctoritati forma constituta est C. Asinio Pollione C. Antistio Vetere cos. anno urbis conditae DCCLXXV. . . . Constitutum (est) ne cui ius esset nisi qui ingenuus ipse, ingenuo patre, avo paterno HS $\overline{\text{CCCC}}$ census fuisset et lege Iulia theatrali in quattuordecim ordinibus sedisset. Postea gregatim insigne id adpeti coeptum. . . . Passimque ad ornamenta ea etiam servitute liberati transiliant, quod antea numquam erat factum, quoniam ferreo anulo et equites iudicesque intellegebantur. Adeoque id promiscuum esse coepit, ut apud Claudium Caesarem in censura eius unus ex equitibus Flavius Proculus CCCC ex ea causa reos postularet. Ita dum separatur ordo ab ingenuis, communicatus est cum servitiis. Iudicum autem appellatione separare eum ordinem primi omnium instituere Gracchi discordi popularitate in contumeliam senatus, mox debellata auctoritas nominis vario seditionum eventu circa publicanos substitit et aliquamdiu tertiae sortis viri publicani fuere. M. Cicero demum stabilivit equestre nomen in consulatu suo Catilinianis rebus, ex eo ordine profectum se celebrans eiusque vires peculiari popularitate quaerens. Ab illo tempore plane hoc tertium corpus in re p. factum est, coepitque adici senatui populoque Romano et equester ordo. Qua de causa et nunc post populum scribitur, quia novissime coeptus est adici.

Vocabulary

adeo adv., to such extent
adicio,-icere,-ieci,-iectum to add
adpeto,-petere,-petivi,-petitum to seek
aliquamdiu adv., for some time
antea adv., before/previously
antiquitas,-atis f., antiquity
C. Antistius,-i Vetus,-i m., consul in A.D. 23 alongside Gaius Asinius Pollio
anulus,-i m., a ring
appellatio,-onis f., title/name
argumentum,-i n., reason
C. Asinius,-i Pollio,-onis m., consul in A.D. 23 alongside Gaius Antistius Vetus. We know from his coins that he was proconsul of Asia. In 45, Pollio was exiled as an accuser of a conspiracy and later was put to death on orders from Empress Valeria Messalina.
auctoritas,-atis f., importance/power conferred/right
aureus,-a,-um golden
aurum,-i n., gold
avus,-i m., grandfather
bellicus,-a,-um warlike
Lucius,-i Brutus,-i m., one of the two first consuls of republican Rome
bulla,-ae f., bulla, a golden ornament of Etruscan origin, worn until age 14–16
Capitolium,-i m., the Capitolium, the temple of Jupiter on the Capitoline Hill
Catilinianus,-a,-um Catilinian/having to do with L. Sergius Catilina, a Roman noble who attempted to take over the state during the consulship of Cicero in 63 B.C.
celebro (1) to extol/boast
censura,-ae f., censorship/office of the censor
census,-us m., property assessment
cerno,cernere,crevi,cretum to perceive
Cicero,-onis m., Marcus Cicero, elected consul in 63 B.C.
circa + acc. applying to
circumago,-agere,-egi,-actum to turn around
Claudius,-i Caesar,-is m., Claudius the emperor of Rome
communico (1) to share with
concilio (1) to procure/bring about
condo,condere,condidi,conditum to found
constat 3rd impers., it is established
constituo,-stituere,-stitui,-stitum to establish/agree upon/decide
consulatus,-us m., consulship
contumelia,-ae f., insult/affront
debellatus,-a,-um debilitated
demum adv., finally
digitus,-i m., finger
discors,-cordis discordant/incongruous
dono (1) to bestow
duro (1) to remain/last/continue
equester,equestris,equestre equestrian
eques,equitis m., citizen of equestrian rank
equidem adv., indeed
Etruscus,-a,-um Etruscan
eventus,-us m., occurrence/event
exterus,-a,-um foreign
fabulosus,-a,-um mythical
fateor,fateri,fassus sum to admit
ferreus,-a,-um of iron
forma,-ae f., a rule/regulation
gemma,-ae f., gemstone
gestamen,-inis n., ornament
Gracchus,-i m., a Roman cognomen, especially referring to Tiberius and Gaius Gracchus the great radical leaders of the late 2nd century B.C.
gregatim adv., in crowds
honoratus,-a,-um honored/noble
ideo adv., for that reason
Iliacus,-a,-um Trojan
induo,induere,indui,indutum + dat. to put on
ingenuus,-a,-um free born
insigne,-is n., distinction/emblem
instituo,-stituere,-stitui,-stitutum + inf. to undertake
intellego,intellegere,intellexi,intellectum to understand/recognize
intra adv., inside
iudex,iudicis m., a judge
Lacedaemon,-onis f., Sparta
legatio,-onis f., a post of duty
legatus,-i m., envoy/legate
lex Iulia theatralis the law establishing specific places to sit for all the classes in theaters, amphitheaters, and circuses
lorum,-i n., a strap of leather
manifestus,-a,-um clear/evident
Midas,Midae m., King Midas of Lydia
mereo,merere,merui,meritum + equo to serve in the cavalry
munus,muneris n., a gift/present
novissime adv., last (in order of events)
Numa,-ae m., Numa Pompilius, 2nd king of Rome
ordo,-dinis m., social order/social class/designated rows of seats in theaters, amphitheaters, and circuses

origo,-ginis f., origin
ornamentum,-i n., distinctive ornament (attached to a rank or office)
passim adv., indiscriminately
paternus,-a,-um paternal
peculiaris,-e particular/specific
plane adv., certainly
popularitas,-atis f., popular support/popularity
postea adv., afterward/subsequently
postulo (1) to prosecute/conduct legal proceedings against
praeter adv., except
praetexta,-ae f., the toga praetexta bordered with purple,worn by boys until they assumed the toga of citizenship
principatus,-us m., rule/reign
proficiscor,profisci,profectus sum to set out/ originate from
Prometheus,-i m., Titan who gave fire to mankind and was chained to a rock in the Caucasus with an iron ring
promiscuus,-a,-um common/indiscriminate
prorsus adv., particularly
publicus,-a,-um public
publicanus,-i m., revenue officer/tax collector
publice adv., officially
quaero,quaerere,quaesivi,quesitum to seek
quamquam conj., although
quia conj., because
quoniam conj., because/since
quoque adv., too (placed after a word for emphasis)
quattuordecim ordines the first 14 rows of theaters, amphitheaters, and circuses reserved for specific property classes by the *lexjulia theatralis*
reus,-i m., defendant/accused person
Romulus,-i m., 1st king of Rome
seditio,-onis f., civil insurrection
sedeo,sedere,sedi,sessum to sit
separo (1) to set apart/distinguish
servitium,-i n., slavery/slaves
servitus,servitutis f., slavery
Servius,-i Tullius,-i m., 5th king of Rome
sinister,-tra,-trum left
siquidem conj., since
sors,sortis f., social ranking/social order
sponsa,-ae f., bride
stabilio,stabilire,stabilivi,stabilitum to stabilize
statua,-ae f., statue
subsisto,-sistere,-stiti to end up/result in applying to
sustineo,-tinere,-tinui,-tentum to hold
Tarquini,-orum m., the Tarquinians; the Etruscan gens from which came two kings of Rome
Tarquinius,-i Priscus,-i m., 4th king of Rome
Tiberius,-i m., the Emperor Tiberius
transilio,transilire,transilui to pass over into
unde adv., from which/whence
ungulus,-i m., digit
unitas,unitatis f., oneness/unity
usus,-us m., use
varius,-a,-um various/diverse
vero adv., indeed
vice (abl. of *vicis*) + **gen.** as a substitute/in place of
vinculum,-i n., fetter/chain

Roman Coinage in Three Metals

Grammar Review

Partitive Genitive
Subjunctive Cum Clauses p. 139

New Grammar

Roman coinage

as,assis = m., as, a copper coin, originally consisting of a pound of copper but frequently reduced in amount and value

sestertius,-i = m., sestertius or sesterce, a Roman silver coin worth 2 and a half *asses.*
*sestert**ium*** (shortened genitive plural) = *sestert**iorum***

Noun clauses introduced by verbs of deciding or resolving take the subjunctive.
The positive conjunction is *ut;* the negative conjunction is *ne* or *ut ne.*

*Constitutum est **ut** asses sextantario pondere ferirentur.*

It was decided **that** asses be struck to a sixth pound.

The Punic Wars

The Punic Wars were a series of three wars fought between Rome and Carthage.
PWI: 264–241 B.C.; PWII: 218–201 B.C.; PWIII: 149–146 B.C.

NB:			
	ac	=	*atque*
	aes alienum		n., national debt
	altera . . . altera		one . . . the other
	maximus,-a,-um		highest (category)
	res p.		res publica

Translation

. . . Servius rex primus signavit aes. Antea rudi usos Romae Timaeus tradit. Signatum est nota pecudum, unde et pecunia appellata. Maximus census $\overline{\text{CXX}}$ assium fuit illo rege, et ideo haec prima classis.

Argentum signatum anno urbis CCCCLXXXV, Q. Ogulnio C. Fabio cos., quinque annis ante primum Punicum bellum. Et placuit 5 denarium pro X libris aeris valere, quinarium pro V, sestertium pro dupondio ac semisse. Librale autem pondus aeris inminutum est bello Punico primo, cum inpensis res p. non sufficeret, constitutumque ut asses sextantario pondere ferirentur. Ita quinque partes lucri factae, dissolutumque aes alienum. Nota aeris eius fuit ex altera parte Ianus geminus, ex altera 10 rostrum navis, in triente vero et quadrante rates. . . .

Vocabulary

aes,aeris n., bronze/a bronze coin
aes alienum n., national debt
altera . . . altera one . . . the other
antea adv., before that time
argentum,-i n., silver
as,assis m., as, a copper coin originally consisting of a pound of copper but this amount was frequently reduced and the coins thus devalued
autem conj., however
census,-us m., property assessment
C. Fabius,-i m., one of the two consuls in 268 B.C.
classis,-is f., a class/social ranking based on wealth into which Servius Tullius divided the whole Roman people
consituo,constiuere,constitui,constitutum to agree upon/decide
denarius,-i m., denarius, a Roman silver coin equal to 10 *asses*
dissolo,-soluere,- solui,-solutum to liquidate
dupondius,-i m., the sum of two asses
ferio,ferire to strike (a coin)/mint
geminus,-a,-um twin faced
ideo adv., for that reason
inminuo,-minuere,-minui,-minutum to reduce in amount
inpensa,-ae f., expenditure
Janus,-i m., the two-faced god of the gates, doorways, and subsequently of beginnings in general
libra,-ae f., Roman pound weight equaling three-fourths of an English pound
libralis,-e (weighing a) pound
lucrum,-i n., material gain/profit
nota,-ae f., design/pattern
pars,partis f., side
pecus,pecudis f., a domestic animal (sheep or cow)
placet,placuit 3rd impers., it is/was agreed
pondus,-eris n., weight

pro adv., for/in proportion to
Punicus,-a,-um Carthaginian
quadrans,-ntis m., quadrans, a Roman coin equivalent to a quarter of an *as*
Q. Ogulnius m., one of the two consuls in 268 B.C.
quinarius,-i m., quinarius, a Roman silver coin equivalent to 5 *asses*
quinque indecl. noun, five
ratis,-is f., ship
rostrum,-i n., beak/bow/ram
rudis,-e raw/unwrought (metal)
semis,-issis m., one half of an as
Servius Tullius m., 578–534 B.C., second of the three Etruscan kings of Rome
sestertius,-i m., sesterce, a Roman silver coin equivalent to 2 and a half *asses*, or a quarter of a denarius
sextantarius,-a,-um a sixth part
signo (1) to stamp (a design on a coin)
sufficio,-ficere,-feci,-fectum + dat. to have sufficient resources
Timaeus,-i m., 356-280 B.C., of Tauromenium (modern Tauromina) in Sicily. His *History* in 38 books was primarily concerned with Sicily, but included events in Italy and Carthage
triens,-ntis n., triens, a Roman coin equivalent to a third of an *as*
valeo,valere,valui,valiturus + pro to be worth/ valued at
vero conj., but indeed

Painting and Portraits

Grammar Review

malo,malle,malui p. 134

New Grammar

NB:	*in aevum*		through the ages/throughout time
	in totum		entirely
	optassent	=	*optavissent*
	similis,-e		correct (in likeness)

Sentences

1. Pictura quondam expetebatur ab regibus sed nunc in totum pulsa est marmoribus, et quidem auro et marmore interraso vermiculatis ad effigies rerum et animalium crustis.

2. Coepimus pingere lapidem, hoc inventum est in principatu Claudii. In principatu Neronis inventum est variare unitatem inserendo maculas, quae non essent in crustis. ut lapis Numidici esset ovatus et lapis Synnadici purpurā distingueretur.

3. Imaginum pictura, qua maxime similes in aevum propagabantur figurae, in totum exolevit. Nunc omnes homines malunt materiam conspici quam se nosci, et pinacothecas veteribus tabulis consuunt alienasque effigies colunt.

Translation

. . . primumque dicemus quae restant de pictura, arte quondam nobili—
tunc cum expeteretur regibus populisque—et alios nobilitante, quos esset
dignata posteris tradere, nunc vero in totum marmoribus pulsa, iam quidem
et auro, nec tantum ut parietes toti operiantur, verum et interraso marmore
vermiculatisque ad effigies rerum et animalium crustis. Non placent iam 5
abaci nec spatia montes in cubiculo dilatantia: coepimus et lapidem pingere.
Hoc Claudii principatu inventum, Neronis vero maculas, quae non essent
in crustis, inserendo unitatem variare, ut ovatus esset Numidicus, ut purpura
distingueretur Synnadicus, qualiter illos nasci optassent deliciae. . . .

Imaginum quidem pictura, qua maxime similes in aevum 10
propagabantur figurae, in totum exolevit. Aerei ponuntur clipei argentea
facie, surdo figurarum discrimine; statuarum capita permutantur. . . . Adeo
materiam conspici malunt omnes quam se nosci, et inter haec pinacothecas
veteribus tabulis consuunt alienasque effigies colunt, ipsi honorem non nisi
in pretio ducentes. . . . Itaque nullius effigie vivente imagines pecuniae, 15
non suas, relinquunt.

Vocabulary

abacus,-i m., panel
adeo adv., to such an extent
aereus,-a,-um bronze
alienus,-a,-um foreign
argenteus,-a,-um silver
caput,capitis n., head
clipeus,-i m., shield
Claudius,-i m., emperor of Rome 41–54 A.D.
colo,colere,colui,cultum to revere/collect
conspico,-spicere,-spexi,-spectum to be noticed/to be the object of attention
consuo,-suere,-sui,-sutum to sew together (into a tapestry)
crusta,-ae f., surface
cubiculum,-i n., bedroom
deliciae,-arum f. pl,. expensive tastes

dignor,dignari,dignatus sum + inf. to deign/ consider worthy
dilato (1) to display
discrimen,discriminis + gen., n., distinction between
distinguo,-tinguere,-tinxi,-tinctum to adorn/ decorate/set off
duco,ducere,duxi,ductum to consider/reckon
effigies,-ei f., likeness
exolesco,-olescere,-olevi,-oletum to become obsolete
expeto,-petere,-petivi,-petitum to seek after/desire
facies,-ei f., face/design
figura,-ae f., figure/likeness
gesto (1) to display
honor,honoris m., distinction/respect/honor
imago,imaginis f., image/picture
insero,-serere,-serui,-sertum to insert/introduce
interrado,-radere,-rasi,-rasum to engrave
lapis,lapidis m., stone
macula,-ae f., a stain/marking
marmor,marmoris n., marble
materia,-ae f., material wealth
mons,montis m., mountain
Nero,Neronis m., Nero Claudius, emperor 54–68 A.D.
nobilis,-e celebrated/illustrious
nobilito (1) to make known/make famous/ennoble
Numidicus,-i, (lapis) m., (stone) quarried in Numidia in North Africa
operio,operire,operui,opertum to cover
opto (1) to desire/choose
ovatus,-a,-um having oval-shaped markings
paries,parietis m., wall
permuto (1) to change out
pictura,-ae f., painting
pinacotheca,-ae f., picture gallery/tapestry
pingo,pingere,pinxi,pictum to draw/paint
pono,ponere,posui,positum to set up as a monument
posteri,-orum m. pl., posterity
pretium,-i n., price
principatus,-us m., rule/principate
propago (1) to extend/transmit
pulsus,-a,-um pushed back in popularity/replaced
purpura,-ae f., purple
qualiter adv., as/just as
quondam adv., formerly/once
resto,restare,restiti to remain
similis,-e correct (in likeness)
spatium,-i n., space
statua,-ae f., statue
surdus,-a,-um faint
Synnadicus,-a,-um Synnadic/of Synnada, in Phrygia in Asia Minor
tabula,-ae f., painting/picture
unitas,unitatis f., sameness/uniformity
vario (1) to vary/give variety to
vermiculatus,-a,-um wavy inlaid
vero conj., but/while
verum et conj., but even/and even
vetus,veteris old/ancient

The Pyramids and the Sphinx

Grammar Review

volo,velle,volui p. 134

New Grammar

Greek proper noun declensions

Nom.	*Bursiris* = f., Bursiris, an ancient town in Egypt	Nom.	*Memphites* = m. adj., belonging to Memphis
Gen.	*Bursiris*	Gen.	*Memphitae*
Dat.	*Bursiri*	Dat.	*Memphitae*
Acc.	*Bursirin*	Acc.	*Memphiten*
Abl.	*Bursire*	Abl.	*Memphite*

Nom.	*Harmais* = m., an ancient king of Egypt
Gen.	*Harmaiae*
Dat.	*Harmaiae*
Acc.	*Harmaian*
Abl.	*Harmaia*

Jussive subjunctives may be used to express duty or obligation and are then translated as "should" or "must."

> ***Dicantur*** *obiter et pyramides in eadem Aegypto.*
>
> And on our journey/in passing pyramids in the same Egypt **must be mentioned**.

Subjunctive clauses introduced by *quippe cum* ("since") are causal.

> . . . ***quippe cum*** *faciendi eas causa a plerisque tradatur . . .*
>
> . . . **since** the cause of making these is recorded by many . . .

Dative of agent occasionally is used with the perfect passive participle.

. . . ***<u>Aegyptiis</u>*** *inter mira ac memoranda narrata.*

. . . recorded **<u>by the Egyptians</u>** among astonishing and notable things

Roman expressions of measurement.
mille passus (1,000 paces) a mile

An overline above Roman numerals indicates a multiplier of 1,000.
$\overline{VII}$ *D* = *VII D passuum* = 7,500 paces, i.e., seven and a half miles

s. = *semis,-issis* = m., half (of anything); *pes,pedis* = m., foot
pedum LXIS = 61 and a half (of) feet

NB:		
	ante + acc.	in front of
	autem	conj., but/however
	causa,-ae	f., reason
	dico,dicere,dixi,dictum	to mention/tell of
	narro (1)	to record/make known
	orbis terrarum	m., the world
	pars,partis	f., side (of the Nile River)
	per + acc.	across
	quippe cum	since
	s. = *semis,-issis*	m., half
	summus,-a,-um	highest/topmost
	vel	even

Sentences

1. Plerique putant pyramides esse ostentationes regum pecuniae.
2. Vestigia complurium incohatarum extant.
3. Una pyramis est in nomo Arsinoite; duae pyramides sunt in nomo Memphite non procul labyrintho.
4. Tres pyramides, quae orbem terrarum inpleverunt fama, sitae sunt IIII milia passuum a Nilo. In vico Bursire adposito, adsueti sunt scandere eas.
5. Ante pyramides est sphinx de qua siluerunt. Sphinx est numen illorum accolentium.
6. Putant Harmaian regem in sphinge conditum esse et volunt videri sphingem invectam esse ad illum locum.

Translation

Dicantur obiter et pyramides in eadem Aegypto, regum pecuniae otiosa ac stulta ostentatio, quippe cum faciendi eas causa a plerisque tradatur, ne pecuniam successoribus aut aemulis insidiantibus praeberent aut ne plebs esset otiosa. Multa circa hoc vanitas hominum illorum fuit. Vestigia complurium incohatarum extant. Una est in Arsinoite nomo, duae in Memphite non procul labyrintho, de quo et ipso dicemus, totidem ubi fuit Moeridis lacus, hoc est fossa grandis, sed Aegyptiis inter mira ac memoranda narrata. Harum cacumina extra aquam eminere dicuntur. Reliquae tres, quae orbem terrarum inplevere fama, sane conspicuae undique adnavigantibus, sitae sunt in parte Africae monte saxeo sterilique inter Memphim oppidum et quod appellari diximus Delta, a Nilo minus IIII milia passuum, a Memphi $\overline{\text{VII}}$ D, vico adposito quem vocant Bursirin; in eo sunt adsueti scandere illas.

Ante est sphinx vel magis narranda, de qua siluere, numen accolentium. Harmaian regem putant in ea conditum et volunt invectam videri; est autem saxo naturali elaborata. Rubrica facies monstri colitur. Capitis per frontem ambitus centum duos pedes colligit, longitudo pedum CCXLIII est, altitudo a ventre ad summam aspidem in capite, LXIS.

Vocabulary

accolo,-colere,-colui,-cultum to live nearby
adnavigo (1) to approach by water (i.e., the Nile River)
adpono,-ponere,-posui,-positum to situate nearby
adsuesco,-suescere,-suevi,-suetum to be accustomed
Aegyptius,-a,-um Egyptian
Aegyptus,-i f., Egypt
aemulus,-i m., rival
altitudino,-onis f., height
ambitus,-us m., circumference
aqua,-ae f., water
Arsinoe,-itis f., a district in Egypt near Suez
aspis,-idis f., asp
Bursiris,-is f., an ancient town in Egypt
cacumen-inis n., summit/tip
circa + acc. about/concerning
colo,-colere,-colui,-cultum to revere/honor/worship
colligo,-ere,-legi,-lectum to be reckoned (in passive)
complures,complurium several
condo,condere,condidi,conditum to bury
conspicuus,-a,-um in sight/visible
Delta indecl., the delta of the Nile
elaboratus,-a,-um carved out
emineo,eminere to stand out/project
exto,-tare,-titi,-itum to be still in existence/to be visible
extra adv., beyond/outside/out of
facies,-ei f., face
fossa,-ae f., excavation
frons, frontis f., forehead
grandis,-e great/vast
Harmais,-ae m., ancient king of Egypt
incohatus,-a,-um unfinished/incomplete
inpleo,inplere,inplevi,inpletum to fill up
insidians,-ntis treacherous
inveho,-vehere,-vexi,-vectum to bring into/import/introduce artificially
labyrinthus,- i m., labyrinth
lacus,-us m., lake
longitudo,-inis f., length
memorandus,-a,-um notable/remarkable
Memphis,-is f., Memphis, a city in Lower Egypt
Memphites,-ae m. adj., of or belonging to Memphis
Moeris,-idis m., Lake Moeris, southwest of Cairo, Egypt, persists today as a smaller lake called Birket Qurun. Lake Moeris was freshwater in prehistory, but is today a saltwater lake. The immense waterworks undertaken by the pharoahs of the 12th Dynasty to transform the lake into a huge water reservoir gave the impression that the lake was an artificial excavation, as reported by classic geographers and travelers.
mirus,-a,-um astonishing
mons,montis m., mountain
monstrum,-i n., legendary creature
narro (1) to record/make known
naturalis,-e natural
Nilus,-i m., Nile River
nomus,-i m., district/province
numen,-inis n., divinity
obiter adv., on the way/in passing
oppidum,-i n., a town
ostentatio,-onis f., vain display/ostentation
otiosus,-a,-um at leisure/unoccupied/superfluous
passus,-us m., pace
pes,pedis m., foot
plebs,plebis f., lower class
plerusque,pleraque,plerumque very many
praebeo,-ere,-ui,-itum to provide/supply
procul adv., at a distance/far
pyramis,-idis f., pyramid
reliquus,-a,-um remaining/the other
ruber,-bra,-brum red/ruddy
sane adv., distinctly/clearly
saxeus,-a,-um rocky
saxum,-i n., rock
scando,scandere,scandi,scansum to climb
sileo,silere,silui to be silent
sino,sinere,sivi,situm to situate/locate
Sphinx,-ngis f., sphinx, mythological monster having a human head and a lion's body
sterilis,-e barren
successor,-oris m., successor
summus,-a,-um highest/topmost
totidem indecl. adj., just as many
undique adv., from all directions
vanitas,-tatis f., vanity
venter,-tris m., belly/stomach
vestigium,-i n., trace/remains
vicus,-i m., town/village

Labyrinths

New Grammar

NB:		
	ab + abl.	prep., after
	dico,dicere,dixi,dictum	to mention/tell about
	iter,itineris	n., passage/walkway
	redeundus,-a,-um	gerundive of *redeo* (to return)
	vel + superlative	by far the most _____

Sentences

1. Etiam nunc est labyrinthus in Aegypto in Heracleopolitis nomo. Traditur Aegyptium labyrinthum factum esse a rege Petesuchi Tithoeve sed Herodotus dicit totum opus esse XII regum novissimique regis Psammetichi.

2. Demoteles dicit regiam Moteridis fuisse, sed Lyceas dicit sepulchrum Moeridis fuisse, plures credunt id exstructum esse sacrum Soli.

3. Non est dubium hinc utique Daedalum sumpsisse exemplar eius labyrinthi quem fecit in Creta, sed imitatum esse tantum centensimam portionem.

4. Continet plures ambages itinerum—occursus ac recursus inexplicabiles crebris foribus inditis ad fallendos redeundumque in errores eosdem.

5. Fecerunt introitum columnasque labyrinthi Aegyptii lapidibus e Paro, reliqua facta sunt e syenite molibus compositis, quas ne saecula quidem possint dissolvere.

Chapter XXIV

Translation

Dicamus et labyrinthos, vel portentosissimum humani inpendii opus, sed
non, ut existimari potest, falsum. Durat etiam nunc in Aegypto in
Heracleopolite nomo qui primus factus est ante annos, ut tradunt, $\overline{\text{III}}$ DC a
Petesuchi rege sive Tithoe, quamquam Herodotus totum opus XII regum
esse dicit novissimique Psammetichi. Causas faciendi varie interpretantur, 5
Demosteles regiam Moteridis fuisse, Lyceas sepulchrum Moeridis, plures
Soli sacrum id exstructum, quod maxime creditur. Hinc utique sumpsisse
Daedalum exemplar eius labyrinthi quem fecit in Creta non est dubium, sed
centensimam tantum portionem eius imitatum, quae itinerum ambages
occursusque ac recursus inexplicabiles continent . . . crebris foribus inditis 10
ad fallendos occursus redeundumque in errores eosdem. Secundus hic fuit
ab Aegyptio labyrinthus, tertius in Lemno, quartus in Italia, omnes lapide
polito fornicibus tecti, Aegyptius, quod miror equidem, introitu lapidibus e
Paro columnisque, reliqua e syenite molibus compositis, quas dissolvere ne
saecula quidem possint. 15

Vocabulary

Aegyptius,-a,-um Egyptian
Aegyptus,-ium f., Egypt
ambages,-is f. pl., a roundabout/circuitous path
centesimus,-a,-um hundredth
columna,-ae f., column/pillar
compono,-ponere,-posui,-positum to arrange/put together in a particular way
creber,crebra,crebrum numerous
Creta,-ae f., Crete, island in the Aegean Sea where beneath the palace of King Minos was the labyrinth containing the Minotaur
Daedalus,-i m., Daedalus, the builder of the labyrinth in Crete
Demosteles,-is m., Demosteles, an ancient author
dico,dicere,dixi,dictum to mention/tell about
dissolvo,-solvere,-solvi,-solutum to dissolve/destroy
dubius,-a,-um uncertain
duro (1) to remain/endure
equidem truly/indeed

error,erroris m., error/wandering about
existimo (1) to think/judge
exstruo,-struere,-struxi,-structum to build
fallo,fallere,fefelli,falsum to deceive/ mislead
falsus,-a,-um fictitious/untrue
foris,foris f., door/entrance
fornix,fornicis m., vault
Heracleopolis,-politis f., a city in Egypt
Herodotus,-i m., the famous 5th-century B.C. Greek historian
hinc adv., here
imitor,imitari,imitatus sum to copy/reproduce
indo,indere,indidi,inditum to place/insert
inexplicabilis,-e inexplicable
inpendium,-i n., public expense
interpretor,interpretari,interpretatus sum to suggest/expound
introitus,-us m., entrance
labyrinthus,-i m., labyrinth/maze
lapis,lapidis m., stone/rock
Lemnos,-i f., a large island in the North Aegean Sea
Lyceas,-ae m., Lyceas of Naucratis, author of a book on Egyptian history
Moeris,Moeridis m., king of Egypt 1818–1770 B.C.
moles,-is f., boulder
Moteris,Moteridis m., ancient king of Egypt, possibly of the 12th Dynasty (1991–1803 B.C.)
nomus,-i m., district
novissimus,-a,-um last
occursus,-us m., blockage/blocked passageway
Paros,-i m., Greek island of the Cyclades, famous for its white marble
Petesuchis,-is m., ancient king of Egypt, possibly of the 12th Dynasty (1991–1803 B.C.)
plures,plura many/several
politus,-a,-um polished/smooth
portentosus,-a,-um abnormal
portio,portionis f., portion
Psammetichus,-i m., ancient king of Egypt of the 26th Dynasty (664–625 B.C.)
quamquam conj., although
recursus,-us m., a return
redeo,-ire,-ii,-itum to return/to be brought back
regia,-ae f., palace
reliquus,-a,-um the other/rest
sacrum,-i n., sacred place/temple
saecula,-orum n. pl., ages of time
secundus,-a,-um next in succession/second
sepulchrum,-i n., tomb
Sol,Solis m., god of the sun
sumo,sumere,sumpsi,sumptum to take (possession) from/adopt
syenites,-is m., a red granite quarried at Syene (now Aswan), a town in Upper Egypt
tantum adv., only
tego,tegere,texi,tectum to cover/roof
Tithoes,-is m., ancient king of Egypt, possibly of the 12th Dynasty (1991–1803 B.C.)
utique adv., at any rate
varie adv., variously/in different ways
vel + superlative by far the most _____

The History of Gemstones

Grammar Review

fero, ferre, tuli, latum p. 133

Compounds: adfero, adferre, attuli, allatum (to bring/bear)
effero, efferre, extuli, elatum (to exalt/elevate)
praefero,-ferre,-tuli,-latum (to display)

New Grammar

1st-declension Greek noun endings

Nom.	*achates* m., an agate
Gen.	*achatae*
Dat.	*achatae*
Acc.	*achaten*
Abl.	*achatea*

NB:

amor,amoris	m., passion/strong desire
auctoritas,auctoritatis	f., high esteem/importance
facio,facere,feci,factum + ostentum	to carry out/fulfill/a prophecy
paria + facio,facere,feci,factum	to square the account/make things equal
in tantum	so much/so entirely
inter initia	in the beginning (of a reign)
primum	adv., for the first time
ratio,-onis	f., the circumstance
vice (abl. of *vicis*) + gen.	in place of

Sentences

1. Fabulae tradunt originem gemmarum anulorumque fuisse a rupe Caucasi. Dicunt fragmentum saxi eius inclusum ferro fuisse primum anulum et primam gemmam.

2. His initiis auctoritas elata est in tantum amorem ut Polycrati tyranno Samio voluntarium damnum unius gemmae videretur esse satis piamenti felicitati adsiduae suae. Si Polycrates lassus adsiduo gaudio hoc unum doluisset, potuisset paria facere cum volubilitate Fortunae.

3. Ergo provectus navigio in altum anulum mersit. At piscis natus eximia magnitudine regi rapiebat illum anulum vice escae et manu Fortunae insidiantis anulum in culina domino rursus reddidit ut faceret ostentum.

4. Constat eam gemmam fuisse sardonychem ostenduntque Romae eandem gemmam (si credimus huic) in aureo cornu in delubro Concordiae, dono Augustae, inclusam et optenentem prope novissimum locum multis praelatis.

5. Dicitur anulum Pyrrhum habuisse achaten anulum in qua novem Musae et Apollo citharam tenens spectarentur, non arte, sed sponte naturae, ita discurrentibus maculis ut singulis Musis sua insignia quoque redderentur.

6. Augustus in eas gemmas sui matris duas similtudinis indiscretae invenit. Altera per bella civilia, absente ipso, amici epistulas et edicta signaverunt.

Chapter XXV

Translation

Quae fuerit origo et a quibus initiis in tantum admiratio haec gemmis exarserit, diximus quadamtenus in mentione auri anulorumque. Fabulae primordium a rupe Caucasi tradunt primumque saxi eius fragmentum inclusum ferro ac digito circumdatum: hoc fuisse anulum et hoc gemmam.

His initiis coepit auctoritas in tantum amorem elata ut Polycrati Samio, insularum ac litorum tyranno, felicitatis suae, quam nimiam fatebatur etiam ipse qui felix erat, satis piamenti in unius gemmae voluntario damno videretur, si cum Fortunae volubilitate paria fecisset, planeque ab invidia eius abunde se redimi putaret, si hoc unum doluisset, adsiduo gaudio lassus. Ergo provectus navigio in altum anulum mersit. At illum piscis, eximia magnitudine regi natus, escae vice raptum, ut faceret ostentum, in culina domino rursus Fortunae insidiantis manu reddidit. Sardonychem eam gemmam fuisse constat, ostenduntque Romae, si credimus, in Concordiae delubro cornu aureo Augustae dono inclusam et novissimum prope locum praelatis multis optinentem.

Post hunc anulum regis alterius in fama est gemma, Pyrrhi illius, qui adversus Romanos bellum gessit. Namque habuisse dicitur achaten in qua novem Musae et Apollo citharam tenens spectarentur, non arte, sed naturae sponte ita discurrentibus maculis ut Musis quoque singulis sua redderentur insignia. . . .

. . . Sulla dictator traditione Iugurthae semper signavit . . . Divus Augustus inter initia sphinge signavit. Duas in matris anulis eas indiscretae similtudinis invenerat. Altera per bella civilia absente ipso signavere amici epistulas et edicta quae ratio temporum nomine eius reddi postulabat, non inficeto lepore accipientium, aenigmata adferre eam sphingem. . . . Augustus 25 postea ad devitanda convicia sphingis Alexandri Magni imagine signavit.

Vocabulary

absens,-ntis absent
abunde adv., more than/completely
achates,-ae m., agate, a volcanic stone with colors ranging from white to gray, light blue, orange to red, black.
adfero,adferre,attuli,allatum to bring/bear
admiratio,-onis f., passion
adsiduus,-a,-um continuous
aenigma,-atis n., enigma/something difficult to explain
alter,altera,alterum the alternate/second
altum,-i n., deep sea
anulus,-i m., ring
Apollo,-inis m., Apollo, god of prophecy, music, poetry, archery, medicine
auctoritas,-atis f., high esteem/importance
Augusta,-ae f., the title given by the Senate to Livia, the wife of Augustus
Augustus,-i m., Augustus Caesar
aureus,-a,-um golden
aurum,-i n., gold
Caucasus,-i m., the Caucasus Mountains west of the Caspian Sea; in mythology, Zeus punished the Titan Prometheus for giving fire to mankind by chaining him to a rock in the Caucasus Mountains and sending an eagle (or vulture) daily to eat his liver
circumdo + dat. (1) to place around
civilis,-e civil
cithara,-ae f., lyre
collatio,-onis f., collection
Concordia,-ae f., temple of Concord in the Forum dedicated to the goddess of peace/harmony/union
constat impers., it is well known/established
convicium-i n., insulting comments/mockery
culina,-ae f., kitchen
damnum,-i n., loss
delubrum,-i n., temple
devito (1) to avoid
dico (1) to dedicate
digitus,-i m., finger
discurro,discurrere,discurri to branch
divus,-a,-um deified
doleo,dolere,dolui,doliturus to suffer
dominus,-i m., master
donec conj., until
edictum,-i n., edict/proclamation
effero,effere,extuli,elatum to exalt/elevate
epistula,-ae f., letter/dispatch
esca,-ae f., bait
etiam conj., indeed
exardesco,-ardescere,-arsi,-arsum to blaze
eximius,-a,-um exceptional/remarkable
fabula,-ae f., story/fable
fama,-ae f., renown
fatalis,-is concerned with fate
felicitas,-atis f., prosperity/happiness
ferrum,-i n., iron
Fortuna,-ae f., goddess of fortune/fate
fragmentum,-i n., fragment
gaudium,-i n., joy/delight
gemma,-ae f., gemstone
imago,-inis f., likeness/image
includo,-cludere,-clusi,-clusum to enclose
indiscretus,-a,-um indistinguishable
inficetus,-a,-um lacking the wit (of seeing the absurdity of the situation)
initium,-i n., beginning
insidior,insidiari to plot/lie in wait
insigne,-is n., emblem/symbol
interpretatio,-onis f., explanation

invidia,-ae f., jealousy/envy
Iugurtha,-ae m., ca. 160–104 B.C., king of Numidia, captured by Sulla
lassus,-a,-um weary/exhausted
lepus,-oris m., joke
litus,-oris n., coast/shore
macula,-ae f., marking
Maecenas,-atis m., right-hand man to Augustus in the arts and domestic policy
magnitudo,-inis f., great size
mentio,-onis f., reference/mention
mergo,mergere,mersi,mersum to plunge in/sink
Musae,-arum f. pl., the nine daughters of Zeus; the goddesses of music, literature, and the arts
namque conj., for
navigium,-i n., boat/ship
nimius,-a,-um excessive
novem nine
novissimus,-a,-um last (in value)
optineo,-tinere,-tinui,-tentum to hold/possess
opinio,-onis f., opinion/belief
origo,-inis f., origin
ostentum,-i n., omen/prophecy
peregrinus,-a,-um foreign
piamentum,-i n., expiation/atonement
piscis,-is m., fish
plane, adv., plainly/clearly
Polycrates,-is m., tyrant of Samos
postea adv., afterward
postulo (1) to demand/require
praefero,-ferre,-tuli,-latum to display
primordium,-i n., origin
primum adv., for the first time
primus,-a,-um first
Prometheus,-i m., Prometheus, the Titan chained to a rock in the Caucasus Mountains by Zeus
prope adv., almost
provectus,-a,-um carried out
Pyrrhus,-i m., the king of Epirus who led mercenary troops into Italy
quadamtenus adv., to a certain extent
quisnam, quidnam who, pray? what, pray?
quippe adv., certainly/to be sure
quique adv., so much the more
rapio,rapere,rapui,raptum to snatch up
ratio,-onis f., circumstances
reddo,reddere,reddidi,redditum to return/render/deliver
redimo,-imere,-emi,-emptum to redeem
rupes,-is f., rocky cliff/crag
rursus adv., back
Samius,-a,-um of Samos
sardonyx,-ychis m., a precious stone with bands of shades of red
saxum,-i n., rock/boulder
scalpo,scalpere,scalpsi,scalptum to engrave
signo (1) to sign (by means of a seal)/stamp (with a seal)
similtudo,-inis f., similarity
singuli,-ae,-a separate/individual
specto (1) to see/view
Sphinx,-ngis f., a mythological monster especially associated with Thebes in Boetia who devoured those who failed to solve its riddle, until Oedipus succeeded in doing so
sponte spontaneously/naturally
Sulla,-ae f., Cornelius Sulla, dictator of Rome 78–82 B.C.
traditio,-onis f., handing over/surrender
vice (abl. of *vicis*) **+ gen.** in place of
vinculum,-i n., fetter/chain
volubilitas,-atis f., inconstancy/fickleness
voluntarius,-a,-um voluntary

Compiled Grammar Charts

Regular Verb Conjugations

Indicative Mood—Active Voice

1st	2nd	3rd	3rd *-io*	4th
		Present		
Vocō	videō	mittō	capiō	sciō
Vocās	vidēs	mittis	capis	scīs
Vocat	videt	mittit	capit	scit
vocāmus	vidēmus	mittimus	capimus	scīmus
vocātis	vidētis	mittitis	capitis	scītis
vocant	vident	mittunt	capiunt	Sciunt
		Imperfect		
vocābam	vidēbam	mittēbam	capiēbam	sciēbam
vocābās	vidēbās	mittēbās	capiēbās	sciēbās
vocābat	vidēbat	mittēbat	capiēbat	sciēbat
vocābāmus	vidēbāmus	mittēbāmus	capiēbāmus	sciēbāmus
vocābātis	vidēbātis	mittēbātis	capiēbātis	sciēbātis
vocābant	vidēbant	mittēbant	capiēbant	Sciēbant
		Future		
vocābō	vidēbō	mittam	capiam	sciam
vocābis	vidēbis	mittēs	capiēs	sciēs
vocābit	vidēbit	mittet	capiet	sciet
vocābimus	vidēbimus	mittēmus	capiēmus	sciēmus
vocābitis	vidēbitis	mittētis	capiētis	sciētis
vocābunt	vidēbunt	mittent	capient	Scient
		Perfect		
vocāvī	vīdī	mīsī	cēpī	scīvī
vocāvistī	vīdistī	mīsistī	cēpistī	scīvistī
vocāvit	vīdit	mīsit	cēpit	scīvit
vocāvimus	vīdimus	mīsimus	cēpimus	scīvimus
vocāvistis	vīdistis	mīsistis	cēpistis	scīvistis
*vocāvērunt	*vīdērunt	*misērunt	*cepērunt	*scīvērunt
	Perfect stem + *ēre* represents an **alternate** 3rd Pl. Perfect form:			
vocavēre	vidēre	misēre	cepēre	scivēre
		Pluperfect		
vocāveram	vīderam	mīseram	cēperam	scīveram
vocāverās	vīderās	mīserās	cēperās	scīverās
vocāverat	vīderat	mīserat	cēperat	scīverat
vocāverāmus	vīderāmus	mīserāmus	cēperāmus	scīverāmus
vocāverātis	vīderātis	mīserātis	cēperātis	scīverātis
vocāverant	vīderant	mīserant	cēperant	scīverant

Future Perfect

vocāverō	vīderō	mīserō	cēperō	scīverō
vocāveris	vīderis	mīseris	cēperis	scīveris
vocāverit	vīderit	mīserit	cēperit	scīverit
vocāverimus	vīderimus	mīserimus	cēperimus	scīverimus
vocāveritis	vīderitis	mīseritis	cēperitis	scīveritis
vocāverint	vīderint	mīserint	cēperint	scīverint

Indicative Mood—Passive Voice

Present

vocor	videor	mittor	capior	scior
vocāris	vidēris	*mitteris	*caperis	scīris
vocātur	vidētur	mittitur	capitur	scītur
vocāmur	vidēmur	mittimur	capimur	scīmur
vocāminī	vidēminī	mittiminī	capiminī	scīminī
vocantur	videntur	mittuntur	capiuntur	sciuntur

Imperfect

vocābar	vidēbar	mittēbar	capiēbar	sciebar
vocābāris	vidēbāris	mittēbāris	capiēbaris	sciēbāris
vocābātur	vidēbātur	mittēbātur	capiēbatur	sciēbātur
vocābāmur	vidēbāmur	mittēbāmur	capiēbamur	sciēbāmur
vocābāminī	vidēbāminī	mittēbāminī	capiēbāminī	sciēbāminī
vocābantur	vidēbantur	mittēbantur	capiēbantur	sciēbantur

Future

vocābor	vidēbor	mittar	capiar	sciar
*vocāberis	*vidēberis	mittēris	capiēris	sciēris
vocābitur	vidēbitur	mittētur	capiētur	sciētur
vocābimur	vidēbimur	mittēmur	capiēmur	sciēmur
vocābiminī	vidēbiminī	mittēminī	capiēminī	sciēminī
vocābuntur	vidēbuntur	mittentur	capientur	scientur

Perfect

vocātus sum	vīsus sum	missus sum	captus sum	scītus sum
vocātus es	vīsus es	missus es	captus es	scītus es
vocātus est	vīsus est	missus est	captus est	scītus est
vocātī sumus	vīsī sumus	mīssī sumus	captī sumus	scītī sumus
vocātī estis	vīsī estis	mīssī estis	captī estis	scītī estis
vocātī sunt	visi sunt	mīssī sunt	captī sunt	scītī sunt

Pluperfect

vocātus eram	visus eram	missus eram	captus eram	scītus eram
vocātus erās	visus erās	mīssus erās	captus erās	scītus erās
vocātus erat	vīsus erat	mīssus erat	captus erat	scītus erat
vocātī erāmus	vīsī erāmus	mīssī erāmus	captī erāmus	scītī erāmus
vocātī erātis	vīsī erātis	mīssī erātīs	captī erātis	scītī erātis
vocātī erant	vīsī erant	mīssī erant	captī erant	sciti erant

Future Perfect

vocātus erō	vīsus erō	mīssus erō	captus erō	scītus erō
vocātus eris	vīsus eris	mīssus eris	captus eris	scītus eris
vocātus erit	vīsus erit	mīssus erit	captus erit	scītus erit
vocātī erimus	vīsī erimus	mīssī erimus	captī erimus	scītī erimus
vocātī eritis	vīsī eritis	mīssī eritis	captī eritis	scītī eritis
vocātī erunt	vīsī erunt	mīssī erunt	captī erunt	scītī erunt

*Consistent Irregular Forms

Subjunctive Mood—Active Voice

Present

vocem	videam	mittam	capiam	sciam
vocēs	videās	mittās	capiās	sciās
vocet	videat	mittat	capiat	sciat
vocēmus	videāmus	mittāmus	capiāmus	sciāmus
vocētis	videātis	mittātis	capiātis	sciātis
vocent	videant	mittant	capiant	sciant

Imperfect

vocārem	viderem	mitterem	caperem	scīrem
vocārēs	vidērēs	mitterēs	caperēs	scīrēs
vocāret	vidēret	mitteret	caperet	scīret
vocārēmus	vidērēmus	mitterēmus	caperēmus	scīrēmus
vocārētis	vidērētis	mitterētis	caperētis	scīrētis
vocārent	vidērent	mitterent	caperent	scīrent

Perfect

vocāverim	vīderim	mīserim	cēperim	scīverim
vocāverīs	vīderīs	mīserīs	cēperīs	scīverīs
vocāverit	vīderit	mīserit	cēperit	scīverit
vocāverīmus	vīderīmus	mīserīmus	cēperīmus	scīverīmus
vocāverītis	vīderītis	miseritis	cēperītis	scīverītis
vocāverint	vīderint	mīserint	cēperint	scīverint

Pluperfect

vocāvissem	vīdissem	misissem	cēpissem	scivissem
vocāvissēs	vīdissēs	misisses	cēpissēs	scīvissēs
vocāvisset	vīdisset	misisset	cēpisset	scīvisset
vocāvissemus	vīdissēmus	mīsissēmus	cepissēmus	scīvissēmus
vocāvissetis	vīdissētis	mīsissētis	cēpissētis	scīvissētis
vocāvissent	vīdissent	mīsissent	cēpissent	scīvissent

Subjunctive Mood—Passive Voice

Present

vocer	vīdear	mittar	capiar	sciar
vocēris	vīdeāris	mittāris	capiāris	sciāris
vocētur	vīdeātur	mittātur	capiātur	sciātur
vocēmur	vīdeāmur	mittāmur	capiāmur	sciāmur
vocēminī	vīdeāminī	mittāminī	capiāminī	sciāminī
vocentur	vīdeantur	mittantur	capiantur	sciantur

Imperfect

vocārer	vīdērer	mitterer	caperer	scīrer
vocārēris	vīdērēris	mitterēris	caperēris	scīrēris
vocārētur	vīdēretur	mitterētur	caperētur	scīrētur
vocārēmur	vīdēremur	mitterēmur	caperēmur	scīrēmur
vocārēminī	vīdēreminī	mitterēminī	caperēminī	scīrēminī
vocārentur	vīdērentur	mitterentur	caperentur	scīrentur

Perfect

vocātus sim	vīsus sim	mīssus sim	captus sim	scitus sim
vocātus sīs	vīsus sīs	mīssus sīs	captus sīs	scitus sīs
vocātus sit	vīsus sit	mīssus sit	captus sit	scītus sit
vocātī sīmus	vīsī sīmus	mīssī sīmus	captī sīmus	scītī sīmus
vocātī sītis	vīsī sītis	mīssī sītis	captī sītis	scītī sītis
vocātī sint	vīsī sint	mīssī sint	capti sint	sciti sint

Pluperfect

vocātus essem	vīsus essem	mīssus essem	captus essem	scītus essem
vocātus essēs	vīsus essēs	mīssus essēs	captus esses	scitus esses
vocātus esset	vīsus esset	mīssus esset	captus esset	scītus esset
vocātī essēmus	vīsī essēmus	mīssī essēmus	captī essēmus	scītī essēmus
vocātī essētis	vīsī essētis	mīssī essētis	captī essētis	scītī essētis
vocātī essent	vīsī essent	mīssī essent	captī essent	scītī essent

Participles

	Active	Passive	Active	Passive
Pres.	vocāns,-ntis		vidēns,-ntis	
Per.		vocātus		vīsus
Fut.	vocātūrus	vocandus (Gerundive)	vīsūrus	videndus (Gerundive)
Pres.	mittēns,-ntis		capiēns,-ntis	
Per.		mīssus		captus
Fut.	mīssūrus	mittendus (Gerundive)	captūrus	capiendus (Gerundive)
Pres.	sciēns,-ntis			
Per.		scītus		
Fut.	scīturus	sciendus (Gerundive)		

Infinitives

	Active	Passive	Active	Passive	Active	Passive
Pres.	vocāre	vocārī	vidēre	viderī	mittere	mittī
Per.	vocāvisse	vocātus esse	vidisse	vīsus esse	mīsisse	mīssus esse
Fut.	vocātūrus esse		vīsūrus esse		mīssūrus esse	

Pres.	capere	capī	scīre	scīrī
Per.	cēpisse	captus esse	scīvisse	scītus esse
Fut.	captūrus esse		scītūrus esse	

Gerunds

Nom.	(vocare)	(videre)	(mittere)	(capere)	(scire)
Gen.	vocandī	videndī	mittendī	capiendī	sciendī
Dat.	vocandō	videndō	mittendō	capiendō	sciendō
Acc.	vocandum	videndum	mittendum	capiendum	sciendum
Abl.	vocandō	videndō	mittendō	capiendō	sciendō

Irregular Verb Conjugations

sum,esse,fuī,futurus to be

Indicative Mood

Pres.	**Imp.**	**Fut.**	**Perf.**	**Plup.**	**Fut.Per.**
sum	eram	erō	fuī	fueram	fuerō
es	erās	eris	fuistī	fuerās	fueris
est	erat	erit	fuit	fuerat	fuerit
sumus	erāmus	erimus	fuimus	fuerāmus	fuerimus
estis	erātis	eritis	fuistis	fuerātis	fueritis
sunt	erant	erunt	fuērunt	fuerant	fuerint

Subjunctive Mood

Pres.	**Imp.**	**Perf.**	**Plup.**
sim	essem	fuerim	fuissem
sīs	essēs	fuerīs	fuissēs
sit	esset	fuerit	fuisset
sīmus	essēmus	fuerīmus	fuissēmus
sītis	essētis	fuerītis	fuissētis
sint	essent	fuerint	fuissent

Infinitives

Pres. esse
Per. fuisse
Fut. futūrus esse/fore

Imperatives

es este

Participles

Fut. futūrus

possum,posse,potuī to be able

Indicative Mood

Pres.	Imp.	Fut.	Perf.	Plup.	FutPer.
possum	poteram	poterō	potuī	potueram	potuerō
potes	poterās	poteris	potuistī	potuerās	potueris
potest	poterat	poterit	potuit	potuerat	potuerit
possumus	poterāmus	poterimus	potuimus	potuerāmus	potuerimus
potestis	poterātis	poteritis	potuistis	potuerātis	potueritis
possunt	poterant	poterunt	potuērunt	potuerant	potuerint

Subjunctive Mood

Pres.	Imp.	Perf.	Plup.
possim	possem	potuerim	potuissem
possīs	possēs	potuerīs	potuissēs
possit	posset	potuerit	potuisset
possīmus	possēmus	potuerīmus	potuissēmus
Possītis	possētis	potuerītis	potuissētis
Possint	possent	potuerint	potuissent

Infinitives

Pres. posse
Perf. potuisse

Participles

Pres. potens,-ntis

eō, īre,iī,itum to go

Indicative Mood

Pres.	Imp.	Fut.	Perf.	Plup.	Fut.Per.
eo	ībam	ībō	Iī	ieram	ierō
īs	ībās	ībis	istī	ierās	ieris
it	ībat	ībit	iit	ierat	ierit
īmus	ībāmus	ībimus	iimus	ierāmus	ierimus
ītis	ībātis	ībitis	istis	ierātis	ieritis
eunt	ībant	ībunt	iērunt	ierant	ierint

Subjunctive Mood

Pres.	Imp.	Perf.	Plup.
eam	īrem	ierim	īssem
eās	īrēs	ierīs	īssēs
eat	īret	ierit	īsset
eāmus	īrēmus	ierīmus	īssēmus
eātis	īrētis	ierītis	īssētis
eant	īrent	ierint	īssent

Infinitives		**Common Participles**		**Imperatives**
Pres.	īre	**Pres.**	iēns,euntis	ī īte
Perf.	isse	**Perf.**	itūm	
Fut.	itūrus esse	**Fut.**	itūrus	**Gerund**
				eundi

ferō,ferre,tulī,lātum to bring/carry/endure/report

Indicative Mood

Active	Passive	Active	Passive	Active	Passive
Present		**Imperfect**		**Future**	
ferō	feror	ferēbam	ferēbar	feram	ferar
fers	ferris	ferēbās	ferēbāris	ferēs	ferēris
fert	fertur	ferēbat	ferēbātur	feret	ferētur
ferimus	ferimur	ferēbāmus	ferēbāmur	ferēmus	ferēmur
fertis	ferimini	ferēbātis	ferēbāminī	ferētis	ferēminī
ferunt	feruntur	ferēbant	ferēbantur	ferent	ferentur
Perfect		**Pluperfect**		**Future Perfect**	
tulī	lātus sum	tuleram	lātus eram	tulerō	lātus erō
tulistī	lātus es	tulerās	lātus erās	tuleris	lātus eris
tulit	lātus est	tulerat	lātus erat	tulerit	lātus erit
tulīmus	lātī sumus	tulerāmus	lātī erāmus	tulerimus	lati erimus
tulīstis	lātī estis	tulerātis	lātī erātis	tuleritis	lati eritis
tulērunt	lātī sunt	tulerant	lātī erant	tulerunt	lati erunt

Subjunctive Mood

Present		**Imperfect**		**Perfect**		**Pluperfect**	
feram	ferar	ferrem	ferrer	tulerim	lātus sim	tulissem	lātus essem
ferās	ferāris	ferrēs	ferrēris	tulerīs	lātus sīs	tulissēs	lātus essēs
ferat	ferātur	ferret	ferrētur	tulerit	lātus sit	tulisset	lātus esset
ferāmus	ferāmur	ferrēmus	ferrēmur	tulerīmus	lātī sīmus	tulissēmus	lātī essēmus
ferātis	ferāminī	ferrētis	ferrēminī	tulerītis	lātī sītis	tulissētis	lātī essētis
ferant	ferantur	ferrent	ferrentur	tulerint	lātī sint	tulissent	lātī essent

	Infinitives		**Participles**		**Imperatives**
	Active	Passive	Active	Passive	fer, ferte
Pres.	ferre	ferrī	ferēns,-ntis		
Per.	tulisse	lātus esse		lātus	
Fut.	lātūrus esse		lātūrus	ferendus	

volō,velle,voluī (to be willing)	**nōlō,nōlle,nōluī** (to be unwilling)	**mālō,mālle,māluī** (to prefer)

Indicative Mood

Present			Imperfect		
volō	nōlō	mālō	volēbam	nōlēbam	mālēbam
vīs	nōn vīs	māvīs	volēbās	nōlēbās	mālēbās
vult	nōn vult	māvult	volēbat	nōlēbat	mālēbat
volumus	nōlumus	mālumus	volēbāmus	nōlēbāmus	mālēbāmus
vultis	nōn vultis	māvultis	volēbātis	nōlēbātis	mālēbātis
volunt	nōlunt	mālunt	volēbant	nōlēbant	mālēbant

Future			Perfect		
volam	nōlam	mālam	voluī	nōluī	māluī
volēs	nōlēs	mālēs	voluistī	nōluistī	māluistī
volet	nōlet	mālet	voluit	nōluit	māluit
volēmus	nōlēmus	mālēmus	voluimus	nōluimus	māluimus
volētis	nōlētis	mālētis	voluistis	nōluistis	māluistis
volent	nōlent	mālent	voluērunt	nōluērunt	māluērunt

Pluperfect			Future Perfect		
volueram	nōlueram	mālueram	voluerō	nōluerō	māluerō
voluerās	nōluerās	māluerās	volueris	nōlueris	mālueris
voluerat	nōluerat	māluerat	voluerit	nōluerit	māluerit
voluerāmus	nōluerāmus	māluerāmus	voluerimus	nōluerimus	māluerimus
voluerātis	nōluerātis	māluerātis	volueritis	nōlueritis	mālueritis
voluerant	nōluerant	māluerant	voluerint	nōluerint	māluerint

Subjunctive Mood

Present			Imperfect		
velim	nōlim	mālim	vellem	nōllem	māllem
velīs	nōlīs	mālīs	vellēs	nōllēs	māllēs
velit	nōlit	mālit	vellet	nōllet	māllet
velīmus	nōlīmus	mālīmus	vellēmus	nōllēmus	māllēmus
velītis	nōlītis	mālītis	vellētis	nōllētis	māllētis
velint	nōlint	mālint	vellent	nōllent	māllent

Perfect			Pluperfect		
voluerim	nōluerim	māluerim	voluissem	nōluissem	māluissem
voluerīs	nōluerīs	māluerīs	voluissēs	nōluissēs	māluissēs
voluerit	nōluerit	māluerit	voluisset	nōluisset	māluisset
voluerīmus	nōluerīmus	māluerīmus	voluissēmus	nōluissēmus	māluissēmus
voluerītis	nōluerītis	māluerītis	voluissētis	nōluissētis	māluissētis
voluerint	nōluerint	māluerint	voluissent	nōluissent	māluissent

Infinitives

Pres.	velle	nōlle	mālle
Per.	voluisse	nōluisse	māluisse

Participles

Pres.	volēns,-ntis	nōlēns,-ntis

Imperatives

noli, nolite

fīō,fierī,factus sum to become/be made/be done

Indicative Mood

Pres.	Imp.	Fut.	Perf.	Plup.	Fut.Per.
fīō	fīēbam	fīam	factus sum	factus eram	factus erō
fīs	fīēbās	fīēs	factus es	factus erās	factus eris
fit	fīēbat	fīet	factus est	factus erat	factus erit
fīmus	fīēbāmus	fīēmus	factī sumus	factī erāmus	facti erimus
fītis	fīēbātis	fīētis	factī estis	factī erātis	facti eritis
fiunt	fīēbant	fient	factī sunt	factī erant	facti erunt

Subjunctive Mood

Pres.	Imp.	Perf.	Plup.
fīam	fierem	factus sim	factus essem
fīās	fierēs	factus sīs	factus essēs
fīat	fieret	factus sit	factus esset
fīāmus	fierēmus	factī sīmus	factī essēmus
fīātis	fierētis	factī sītis	factī essētis
fīant	fierent	factī sint	factī essent

Participles		Infinitives	Imperatives
Pres.		fierī	fī fīte
Perf.	factus,-a,-um	factus esse	
Fut.	faciendus,-a,-um	[factum īrī]	

Deponent Verb Conjugations

1st	hortor,	hortārī,	hortātus sum	to urge
2nd	fateor,	faterī,	fassus sum	to confess
3rd	sequor,	sequī,	secutus sum	to follow
3rd -io	morior,	morī,	mortuus sum	to die
4th	orior,	orīrī,	ortus sum	to arise

Indicative Mood

Present

hortor	fateor	sequor	morior	orior
hortāris	fatēris	sequeris	moreris	orīrīs
hortātur	fatētur	sequitur	moritur	orītur
hortāmur	fatēmur	sequimur	morimur	orīmur
hortāminī	fatēminī	sequimini	morimini	orīminī
hortantur	fatentur	sequuntur	moriuntur	oriuntur

Imperfect

hortābar	fatēbar	sequēbar	moriēbar	oriēbar
hortābāris	fatēbāris	sequēbāris	moriēbāris	oriēbāris
hortābātur	fatēbātur	sequēbātur	moriēbātur	oriēbātur
hortābāmur	fatēbāmur	sequēbāmur	moriēbāmur	oriēbāmur
hortābāminī	fatēbāminī	sequēbāminī	moriēbāminī	oriēbāminī
hortābantur	fatēbantur	sequēbantur	moriēbantur	oriēbantur

Future

hortābor	fatēbor	sequar	moriar	oriar
hortāberis	fatēberis	sequēris	moriēris	oriēris
hortābitur	fatēbitur	sequētur	moriētur	oriētur
hortābimur	fatēbimur	sequēmur	moriēmur	oriēmur
hortābiminī	fatēbiminī	sequēminī	moriēminī	oriēminī
hortābuntur	fatēbuntur	sequentur	morientur	orientur

Perfect

hortātus sum	fassus sum	secūtus sum	mortuus sum	ortus sum
hortātus es	fassus es	secūtus es	mortuus es	ortus es
hortātus est	fassus est	secūtus est	mortuus est	ortus est
hortātī sumus	fassī sumus	secūtī sumus	mortuī sumus	ortī sumus
hortātī estis	fassī estis	secūtī estis	mortuī estis	ortī estis
hortātī sunt	fassī sunt	secūtī sunt	mortuī sunt	ortī sunt

Pluperfect

hortātus eram	fassus eram	secūtus eram	mortuus eram	ortus eram
hortātus erās	fassus erās	secūtus erās	mortuus erās	ortus erās
hortātus erat	fassus erat	secūtus erat	mortuus erat	ortus erat
hortātī erāmus	fassī erāmus	secutā erāmus	mortuī erāmus	orti eramus
hortātī erātis	fassī erātis	secutī erātis	mortuī erātis	ortī erātis
hortātī erant	fassī erant	secūtī erant	mortuī erant	ortī erant

Future Perfect

hortātus ero	fassus erō	secūtus erō	mortuus erō	ortus erō
hortātus eris	fassus eris	secūtus eris	mortuus eris	ortus eris
hortātus erit	fassus erit	secūtus erit	mortuus erit	ortus erit
hortātī erimus	fassī erimus	secūtī erimus	mortuī erimus	ortī erimus
hortātī eritis	fassī eritis	secūtī eritis	mortuī eritis	ortī eritis
hortātī erunt	fassī erunt	secūtī erunt	mortuī erunt	ortī erunt

Subjunctive Mood

Present

horter	fatear	sequar	moriar	oriar
hortēris	fateāris	sequāris	moriāris	oriāris
hortētur	fateātur	sequātur	moriātur	oriātur
hortēmur	fateāmur	sequāmur	moriāmur	oriāmur
hortēminī	fateāminī	sequāminī	moriāminī	oriāminī
hortentur	fateantur	sequantur	moriantur	oriantur

Imperfect

hortārer	fatērer	sequerer	morerer	orīrer
hortārēris	fatērēris	sequerēris	morerēris	orīrēris
hortārētur	fatērētur	sequerētur	morerētur	orīrētur
hortārēmur	fatērēmur	sequerēmur	morerēmur	orīrēmur
hortārēminī	fatērēminī	sequerēminī	morerēminī	orīrēminī
hortārentur	fatērentur	sequerentur	morerentur	orīrentur

Perfect

hortātus sim	fassus sim	secūtus sim	mortuus sim	ortus sim
hortātus sīs	fassus sīs	secūtus sīs	mortuus sīs	ortus sīs
hortātus sit	fassus sit	secūtus sit	mortuus sit	ortus sit
hortātī sīmus	fassī sīmus	secūtī sīmus	mortuī sīmus	orti simus
hortātī sītis	fassī sītis	secūtī sītis	mortuī sītis	ortī sītis
hortātī sint	fassī sint	secūtī sint	mortuī sint	ortī sint

Pluperfect

hortātus essem	fassus essem	secūtus essem	mortuus essem	ortus essem
hortātus essēs	fassus essēs	secūtus essēs	mortuus essēs	ortus essēs
hortātus esset	fassus esset	secūtus esset	mortuus esset	ortus esset
hortātī essēmus	fassī essēmus	secūtī essēmus	mortuī essēmus	ortī essēmus
hortātī essētis	fassī essētis	secūtī essētis	mortuī essētis	ortī essētis
hortātī essent	fassī essent	secūtī essent	mortuī essent	ortī essent

Participles

Active

Pres.	hortāns,-ntis	fatēns,-ntis	sequēns,-ntis	moriēns,-ntis	oriēns,-ntis
Per.	hortātus	fassus	secūtus	mortuus	ortus
Fut.	hortātūrus	fassūrus	secūtūrus	moritūrus	ortūrus

Passive

Fut.	hortandus	fatendus	sequendus	moriendus	oriendus

Infinitives

Pres.	hortārī	fatērī	sequī	morī	orīrī
Per.	hortātus esse	fassus esse	secūtus esse	mortuus esse	ortus esse
Fut.	hortātūrus esse	fassūrus esse	secūtūrus esse	moritūrus esse	ortūrus esse

Imperatives

Sing.	hortāre	fatēre	sequere	morere	orīre
Pl.	hortāminī	fatēminī	sequimini	morimini	orīminī

Compiled Chart of Major Subjunctive Usages

Independent Usages

	Translation	Negative
1. **Jussive**	"Let"	**Nē** "Let not"

Regarded as a soft command; always in the present tense, most frequently in 3rd person.

Dicat sibi.	Let him speak for himself.
Servi hoc faciant.	Let the slaves do this.

2. **Optative**	"May"	***Nē*** "May . . . not"

Used in expressions of wishing.

Respiciat in pace.	May he rest in peace.
Ne semper sit hoc verum.	May this not always be true.

When used with past tenses, regularly accompanied by ***utinam*** (Would that! O that!)

Utinam studuissem!	Would that I had studied!

3. Other somewhat common independent usages:

1) Hortatory	*Eamus!*	Let's go!
2) Deliberative	*Redeam?*	Should I go back?*

*rhetorical question

Dependent Usages

Subjunctive Sequence of Tenses

Independent Main Verb	Dependent Subjunctive Verb	
Present or Future Tense	Present Subjunctive	Same Time or Time After
	Perfect Subjunctive	Time Before
Any Past Tense	Imperfect Subjunctive	Same Time or Time After
	Pluperfect Subjunctive	Time Before

1. **Purpose Clauses**	Pos. Conj.	Neg. Conj.
	ut *"in order that"*	***nē*** "lest/in order that not"
Facit hoc ut urbem servet.	He does this to save the city.	
Fecit hoc ne urbs deleretur.	He did this lest the city was destroyed.	

2. **Result Clauses**	Cue Words	Pos. Conj.	Neg. Conj.
	ita,sic,tam "so"	***ut*** "that"	***ut nōn*** "that . . . not"
	tantus,-a,-um		***ut nemo*** "that no one"
	"such great"		***ut nihil*** "that nothing"

Fecit tanta ut urbem servaret.
He did such great things that he saved the city.
Historia erat ita stulta ut nemo ei crederet.
The story was so foolish that no one believed it.

Result by Context	Cue Verbs	Pos. Conj.	Neg. Conj.
	accido	***(ut)*** "that"	***ut non*** "that not"
	evenio		***ut nemo*** "that no one"
	efficio		***ut nihil*** "that nothing"

Evenit ut nihil factum esset. It turned out that nothing had been done.

3. ***Cum* Clauses**
   Cum followed by a subjunctive verb may be translated as "when, since, although." When ***tamen*** occurs in the main clause, *cum* is always translated "**although**."
   Cum scirent hoc, discipuli erant feliciores.
   When they understood this, the students were happier.
   Cum pericula videret, tamen venit.
   Although he understood the dangers, nevertheless he came.

4. **Indirect Questions**
   Indirect questions are introduced by verbs of "asking, perceiving, knowing" and "thinking," followed by an interrogative pronoun, adverb or adjective cue word.
   Common interrogative cue words: ***quis?quid? qui?quae?quod? cūr? ubi? an? utrum . . . an? uter,-tra,-trum? quomodo?quam? quantus,-a,-um?***

Rogavit ubi fuisses.	He asked where you had been.
Scit quis hoc fecerit.	He knows who did this.

5. **Jussive Noun Clauses**
   Introductory cue verbs: ***rogo, curo, moneo, hortor, oro, peto***

Pos. Conj.: ***ut*** "to . . . /that"	Neg. Conj.: ***nē*** "not to . . . /that . . . not"
Monui eum ut veniret.	I advised him to come.
Rogo a te ne facias hoc.	I beg you not to do this.
Cura ut venias.	Take care that you come.

6. **Conditional Statements** Pos. Conj.: ***si*** Neg. Conj.: ***nisi***

   1) **Less Likely** "**should/would**"
   Verb form: present subjunctive/present subjunctive

Si hoc facias, sis beatior.	Should you do this, you would be happier.
Nisi facias, sis miserior.	Should you not do this, you would be rather wretched.

   2) **Contrary to Fact in the Present** "**were/would**"
   Verb form: imperfect subjunctive/imperfect subjunctive

Si ego essem tu, facerem hoc.	If I were you, I would do this.
Nisi esset amicus, non faceremus hoc.	Were he not a friend, we would not do this.

   3) **Contrary to Fact in the Past** "**had/would have**"
   Verb form: pluperfect subjunctive/pluperfect subjunctive
   Si venisset, urbs non amissa esset.
   Had he come, the city would not have been lost.
   Nisi egisset subito, omnes mortuui essent.
   Had he not acted immediately, all would have died.

7. **Relative Clauses of Characteristic**

Introductory cue phrases:	***quis est qui, nemo est qui, quid est quod,sunt qui, sunt quae, solus est qui***
Quis est qui credat hoc?	Who is there who would believe this?
Sunt qui faciant hoc.	There are (men) who would do this.

8. **Subordinate Clauses in Indirect Statement**
   Nescivit viros qui dixissent haec abisse.
   He did not know that the men who had said these things had gone away.

9. **Noun Clauses following Verbs** of "fearing, preventing, refusing, doubting" and other subjective thoughts represent the possibility of subjunctive verbs.

Noun Declensions

1st-Declension Nouns

puella,-ae = f., girl

	Sing.	Pl.
Nom.	puella	puellae
Gen.	puellae	puellārum
Dat.	puellae	puellīs
Acc.	puellam	puellās
Abl.	puellā	puellīs
Voc.	puella	puellae

2nd-Declension Nouns

Nominative Ending in ***-ius***

	filius,- ī = m., son		*amicus,- ī* = m., friend	
	Sing.	Pl.	Sing.	Pl.
Nom.	filius	filiī	amīcus	amicī
Gen.	filiī	filiōrum	amīcī	amicōrum
Dat.	filiō	filiīs	amīcō	amicīs
Acc.	filium	filiōs	amīcum	amicōs
Abl.	filiō	filiīs	amīcō	amicīs
Voc.	filī	filiī	amice	amicī

2nd-Declension Nouns

Nominative Ending in ***-ir*** or ***-er***

	vir,virī = m., man		*ager,agrī* = m., field	
	Sing.	Pl.	Sing.	Pl.
Nom.	vir	virī	ager	agrī
Gen.	virī	virōrum	agrī	agrōrum
Dat.	virō	virīs	agrō	agrīs
Acc.	virum	virōs	agrum	agrōs
Abl.	virō	virīs	agrō	agrīs
Voc.	vir	virī	ager	agrī

Neuter 2nd-Declension Nouns

dōnum,- ī = n., gift

	Sing.	Pl.
Nom.	dōnum	dōna
Gen.	dōnī	dōnōrum
Dat.	dōnō	dōnīs
Acc.	dōnum	dōna
Abl.	dōnō	dōnīs
Voc.	dōnum	dōna

3rd-Declension Nouns

	rēx,rēgis = m., king		*pāx,pācis* = f., peace		*tempus,temporis* = n., time	
	Sing.	Pl.	Sing.	Pl.	Sing.	Pl.
Nom.	rēx	regēs	pāx	pācēs	tempus	tempora
Gen.	rēgis	regum	pācis	pācum	temporis	temporum
Dat.	rēgī	regibus	pācī	pācibus	temporī	temporibus
Acc.	rēgem	regēs	pācem	pācēs	tempus	tempora
Abl.	rēge	regibus	pāce	pācibus	tempore	temporibus

3rd-Declension *i*-stem Nouns

	1. Parisyllabics		**2. Consonant Base**	
	cīvis,cīvis = m., citizen		*ars,artis* = f., ant/skill	
Nom.	cīvis	cīvēs	ars	artes
Gen.	cīvis	cīvium	artis	artium
Dat.	cīvī	cīvibus	arti	artibus
Acc.	cīvem	cīvēs	artem	artes
Abl.	cīve	cīvibus	arte	artibus

3. Neuters Ending in *-e,-al,-ar*

	mare,maris = n., sea		*animal,animalis* n., = animal	
Nom.	mare	maria	animal	animalia
Gen.	maris	marium	animalis	animalium
Dat.	marī	maribus	animalī	animalibus
Acc.	mare	maria	animal	animalia
Abl.	marī	maribus	animali	animalibus

exemplar,exemplaris = n., example/model

Nom.	exemplar	exemplaria
Gen.	exemplaris	exemplarium
Dat.	exemplarī	exemplaribus
Acc.	exemplar	exemplaria
Abl.	exemplarī	exemplaribus

	4th-Declension Nouns				**5th-Declension Nouns**	
	exercitus,exercitus = m., army		*cornu,cornus* = n., horn		*res,rei* = f., thing	
Nom.	exercitus	exercitūs	cornū	cornua	rēs	rēs
Gen.	exercitūs	exercituum	cornūs	cornuum	reī	rērum
Dat.	exercituī	exercitibus	cornū	cornibus	reī	rēbus
Acc.	exercitum	exercitūs	cornū	cornua	rem	rēs
Abl.	exercitū	exercitibus	cornū	cornibus	rē	rēbus

Irregular Nouns

	nemo,neminis = m./f., no one	***vis,vis*** = f., force; pl.= strength	
Nom.	nemo	vis	virēs
Gen.	neminis	vis	virium
Dat.	nemini	vi	viribus
Acc.	neminem	vim	virēs
Abl.	nullo/nulla	vi	viribus

	deus,dei = m., god	
Nom.	deus	dei or di
Gen.	dei	deorum
Dat.	deo	deis or dis
Acc.	deum	deos
Abl.	deo	deis or dis

Pronouns

Demonstrative Pronouns

	hic,haec,hoc this, the latter			*ille,illa,illud* that, the former		
	m.	f.	n.	m.	f.	n.
Nom.	hic	haec	hoc	ille	illa	illud
Gen.	huius	huius	huius	illius	illius	illius
Dat.	huic	huic	huic	illī	illī	illī
Acc.	hunc	hanc	hoc	illum	illam	illud
Abl.	hōc	hāc	hōc	illō	illā	illō
Nom.	hī	hae	haec	illi	illae	illa
Gen.	hōrum	hārum	hōrum	illōrum	illārum	illōrum
Dat.	hīs	hīs	hīs	illīs	illīs	illīs
Acc.	hōs	hās	haec	illōs	illās	illa
Abl.	hīs	hīs	hīs	illīs	illīs	illīs

iste,ista,istud such/that of yours

Nom.	iste	ista	istud	istī	istae	ista
Gen.	istius	istius	istius	istōrum	istārum	istōrum
Dat.	istī	istī	istī	istīs	istīs	istīs
Acc.	istum	istam	istud	istōs	istās	ista
Abl.	istō	istā	istō	istīs	istīs	istīs

Intensive Pronoun

ipse,ipsa,ipsum himself,herself,itself

Nom.	ipse	ipsa	ipsum	ipsī	ipsae	ipsa
Gen.	ipsius	ipsius	ipsius	ipsōrum	ipsārum	ipsōrum
Dat.	ipsī	ipsī	ipsī	ipsīs	ipsīs	ipsīs
Acc.	ipsum	ipsam	ipsum	ipsōs	ipsās	ipsa
Abl.	ipsō	ipsā	ipsō	ipsīs	ipsīs	ipsīs

Personal Pronouns

	1st Person		**2nd Person**	
Nom.	***ego*** I	***nōs*** we	***tū*** you	***vōs*** you
Gen.	mei	nostrum/nostri	tuī	vestrum/vestri
Dat.	mihi	nōbis	tibi	vōbis
Acc.	mē	nōs	tē	vōs
Abl.	mē	nōbis	tē	vōbis

3rd Person

Nom.	***is*** he	***ea*** she	***id*** it	**eī**	**eae**	**ea**
Gen.	eius	eius	eius	eōrum	eārum	eōrum
Dat.	eī	eī	eī	eīs	eīs	eīs
Acc.	eum	eam	id	eōs	eās	ea
Abl.	eō	eā	eō	eīs	eīs	eīs

Reflexive Pronouns

1st Person

	Sing.		Pl.
Nom.	—		—
Gen.	mei *of myself*	nostrum/nostri	*of ourselves*
Dat.	mihi		nōbis
Acc.	mē		nōs
Abl.	mē		nōbis

2nd Person

Nom.	—		—
Gen.	.	tuī *of yourself*	vestrum/vestri *of yourselves*
Dat.	tibi		vōbis
Acc.	tē		vōs
Abl.	tē		vōbis

3rd Person

(same form for singular and plural)

Nom.	—
Gen.	suī *of himself/herself/itself/themselves*
Dat.	sibi
Acc.	sē
Abl.	sē

Interrogative Pronouns

	m./f.	n.	m.	f.	n.
Nom.	*quis* who?	*quid* what?	quī	quae	quae
Gen.	cuius	cuius	quōrum	quārum	quōrum
Dat.	cui	cui	quibus	quibus	quibus
Acc.	quem	quid	quōs	quās	quae
Abl.	quō	quō	quibus	quibus	quibus

Relative Pronouns

	m.	f.	n.
Nom.	*quī* who	*quae* who	*quod* that/which
Gen.	cuius	cuius	cuius
Dat.	cui	cui	cui
Acc.	quem	quam	quod
Abl.	quō	quā	quō
Nom.	quī	quae	quae
Gen.	quōrum	quārum	quōrum
Dat.	quibus	quibus	quibus
Acc.	quōs	quās	quae
Abl.	quibus	quibus	quibus

NB: When ***cum*** is used with the **ablative forms** of the above pronouns, it is attached to the end: ***mēcum, tēcum, sēcum, nōbiscum, vōbiscum, quōcum,quācum,quibuscum***.

Irregular Pronoun *idem,eadem,idem*

idem,eadem,idem = the same

	Singular			Plural		
	m.	f.	n.	m.	f.	n.
Nom.	īdem	eadem	idem	eidem	eaedem	eadem
Gen.	eiusdem	eiusdem	eiusdem	eōrundem	eārundem	eōrundem
Dat.	eīdem	eīdem	eīdem	eīsdem	eīsdem	eīsdem
Acc.	eundem	eandem	idem	eōsdem	eāsdem	eadem
Abl.	eōdem	eādem	eōdem	eīsdem	eīsdem	eīsdem

Adjectives

1st–2nd Declension *bonus,-a,-um* good

	m.	f.	n.	m.	f.	n.
Nom.	bonus	bona	bonum	bonī	bonae	bona
Gen.	bonī	bonae	bonī	bonōrum	bonārum	bonōrum
Dat.	bonō	bonae	bonō	bonīs	bonīs	bonīs
Acc.	bonum	bonam	bonum	bonōs	bonās	bona
Abl.	bonō	bonā	bonō	bonīs	bonīs	bonīs
Voc.	bone	bona	bonum	bonī	bonae	bona

Irregular 1st–2nd Declension Adjectives (*alter,nullus,unus,totus,solus,ullus*)

Nom.	ūllus	ūlla	ūllum	ūllī	ūllae	ūlla
Gen.	ūllius	ūllius	ūllius	ūllōrum	ūllārum	ūllōrum
Dat.	ūllī	ūllī	ūllī	ūllīs	ūllīs	ūllīs
Acc.	ūllum	ūllam	ūllum	ūllōs	ūllās	ūlla
Abl.	ūllō	ūllā	ūllō	ūllīs	ūllīs	ūllīs

3rd-Declension Adjective of Three Endings: *celer,celeris,celere* = swift/fast

Nom.	celer	celeris	celere	celerēs	celerēs	celeria
Gen.	celeris	celeris	celeris	celerium	celerium	celerium
Dat.	celerī	celerī	celerī	celeribus	celeribus	celeribus
Acc.	celerem	celerem	celere	celerēs	celerēs	celeria
Abl.	celerī	celerī	celerī	celeribus	celeribus	celeribus

3rd-Declension Adjective of Two Endings: *omnis,-e* = every/all

	m./f.		n.	
Nom.	omnis	omnēs	omne	omnia
Gen.	omnis	omnium	omnis	omnium
Dat.	omnī	omnibus	omnī	omnibus
Acc.	omnem	omnēs	omne	omnia
Abl.	omnī	omnibus	omnī	omnibus

3rd-Declension Adjective of One Ending: *fēlix,fēlīcis* = happy

Nom.	fēlix	fēlīcēs	fēlix	fēlīcia
Gen.	fēlīcis	fēlīcium	fēlīcis	fēlīcium
Dat.	fēlīcī	fēlīcibus	fēlīcī	fēlīcibus
Acc.	fēlīcem	fēlīces	fēlix	fēlīcia
Abl.	fēlīcī	fēlīcibus	fēlīcī	fēlīcibus

Possessive Adjectives

1st Person	meus,-a,-um *my*	noster,nostra,nostrum *our*
2nd Person	tuus,-a,-um *your*	vester,vestra,vestrum *your*
3rd Person (Reflexive)	suus,-a,-um *his own,her own, its own*	suus,-a,-um *their own*

Interrogative Adjectives

	m.	f.	n.	m.	f.	n.
Nom.	*quī* which?	*quae* which?	*quod* which?	quī	quae	quae
Gen.	cuius	cuius	cuius	quōrum	quārum	quōrum
Dat.	cui	cui	cui	quibus	quibus	quibus
Acc.	quem	quam	quod	quōs	quās	quae
Abl.	quō	quā	quō	quibus	quibus	quibus

Regular Comparative and Superlative Adjectives and Adverbs

Positive	**Comparative**	**Superlative**
clarus,-a,-um	clarior, clarius	clarissimus
clare	clarius	clarissime
pulcher,-chra,-chrum	pulchrior, pulchrius	pulcherrimus
pulchre	pulchrius	pulcherrime
fortis,-e	fortior,fortius	fortissimus
fortiter	fortius	fortissime
similis,-e	similior,similius	simillimus
similiter	similius	simillime

Common Irregular Adjectives and Adverbs

Positive	**Comparative**	**Superlative**
bonus,-a,-um	melior, melius	optimus,-a,-um
bene	melius	optime
magnus,-a,-um	maior, maius	maximus,-a,-um
magnopere	magis	maxime
malus,-a,-um	peior, peius	pessimus,-a,-um
male	peius	pessime
parvus,-a,-um	minor, minus	minimus,-a,-um
parum	minus	minime
multus,-a,-um	plures, plura	plurimus,-a,-um
multum	plus	plurimum
facilis,-e	facilior, facilius	facillimus,-a,-um
facile	facilius	facillime
diu	diutius	diutissime
saepe	saepius	saepissime

Common Correlatives

alii . . . alii	*some . . . others*
aut . . . aut	*either . . . or*
cum . . . tum	*while . . . .at the same time*
et . . . et	*both . . . and*
neque (nec) . . . neque (nec)	*neither. . . .nor*
ne . . . .quidem	*not even*
non solum . . . sed etiam	*not only . . . but also*
quam . . . tam	*how much . . . so much*
quotiens . . . totiens	*as often as . . . so often as*
sive . . . sive	*if . . . or if*
tum . . . tum	*not only . . . but also*
utrum . . . an	*whether . . . or*
vel . . . vel	*either . . . or*

Major Ablative Uses

1. Ablative of **Time When**	*unā horā*	in one hour
	eō tempore	at that time

The ablative of time when is never introduced by a preposition, always contains a noun referring to time, and is translated *in* or *at*.

2. Ablative of **Place Where**	*in colosseō*	in the colosseum
	in forō	in the forum

The ablative of place where is always preceded by the preposition ***in*** and answers the question "where."

3. Ablative of **Place from Which**	*ē periculō*	out of danger
	ā bellō	away from the war
	dē urbe	from the city

The ablative of place from which is introduced by the prepositions ***ab, de***, or ***ex*** and indicates motion away from a person, place, or thing.

4. Ablative of **Accompaniment**	*cum amīcō*	with a friend
	cum puellā	with the girl

The ablative of accompaniment is always preceded by the preposition ***cum*** and answers the question "with whom."

5. Ablative of **Manner**	*cum laude*	with praise
	magnā cum laude	with great praise
	magnā laude	with great praise

The ablative of manner answers the question "how" and must be preceded by ***cum*** unless used with an adjective, in which case the use of ***cum*** is optional. Note that if ***cum*** is used with an adjective that ***cum*** falls between the noun and adjective.

6. Ablative of **Means**	*pecuniā*	by means of money
	gladiō	by means of a sword

The ablative of means usually occurs as a single word ablative without a preposition and answers the question "with what" or "by (means of) what."

7. Ablative of **Agent** | *Factum est ab eō.* | It was done by him
   The ablative of agent occurs only with passive verbs and tells "by whom" an action is done.

8. Ablative of **Separation** | *Caret pecuniā.* | He lacks money.
   Liberantur metū. | They are free from fear.
   The ablative of separation follows verbs of freeing (*līberō*), lacking (*careō*), or depriving (*prīvō*).

9. Ablative **Absolute**
   Iuribus scitis, poena erat clara. | Since the laws were known, the punishment was clear.
   Caesare tenente imperium, non timebo. | With Caesar holding the command, I will not fear.

The ablative absolute consists of a noun or pronoun in the ablative case with a participle agreeing. An ablative absolute may not modify a noun or a pronoun in the main clause of a sentence.

Glossary

ab (ā) + abl. from/away from/by
abeō,abīre,abiī,abitum to go away/depart
ac/atque and/and also/and even
accido,accidere,accidi to happen
accipiō,accipere,accēpī,acceptum to take/accept
ācer,ācris,ācre sharp/fierce/keen
acerbus,-a,-um harsh/bitter
ad + acc. acc. toward/to (with verbs of motion)
adulēscens,adulēscentis m., youth/adolescent
adversum + acc. against
adversus,-a,-um adverse
aequus,-a,-um level/even/equal/just
aetās,aetātis f., age/period of life
ager,agrī m., field
agō,agere,ēgī,āctum to do/lead/act/drive
agricola,-ae m., farmer
ait,aiunt defective verb; he says/they say
aliquis,aliquid someone/something
alius,alia,aliud another/other
alō,alere,aluī,altum to support/nourish/sustain
amīca,-ae, f., friend
amīcitia,-ae f., friendship
amīcus,-ī m., friend
āmittō,āmittere,āmīsī,āmissum to lose
amō (1) to love
amor,amōris m., love
an whether/or
animal,animalis n., animal
animus,-ī m., soul/spirit; pl., pride/courage
annus,-ī m., year
ante + acc. before
antepōnō,-pōnere,-posuī,-positum to prefer/put before
antīquus,-a,-um old/ancient
appellō (1) to call/name
apud + acc. among/in the presence of/at the house of
arbitror,arbitrārī,arbitratus sum to judge/think
arma,armōrum n. pl., weapons/arms
ars,artis f., art/skill
Asia,-ae f., Asia
at but
Athēnae,-ārum f. pl., Athens
atque/ac and/and also/and even
auctor,auctōris m., author
audeō,audēre,ausus sum to dare
audiō,audīre,audīvī,audītum to hear/listen
aut or
aut . . . aut either . . . or
autem moreover/however
auxilium,-ī n., help/aid
beātus,-a,-um blessed/happy/fortunate
bellum,-ī n., war
bellus,-a,-um pretty
bene adv., well
beneficium,-ī n., favor/kindness/benefit
bonus,-a,-um good
brevis,-e brief
caelum,-ī n., sky/heaven
Caesar,Caesaris m., Caesar
canis,-is c., dog
caput,capitis n., head
capiō,capere,cēpī,captum to capture/seize
careō,carēre,caruī,caritūrus + abl. of sep. to lack/be deprived of
Carthāgō (Karthāgō),-inis f., Carthage
cārus,-a,-um dear
causa,-ae f., cause/reason/case; **gen. + causā** for the sake of/on account of
cēdō,cēdere,cessī,cessum to yield/withdraw or go by/proceed
celer,celeris,celere swift/quick/rapid
cēna,-ae f., dinner
cēnō (1) to dine
certus,-a,-um certain
cēterī,-ae,-a the rest/the other
Cicero,Ciceronis m., Cicero
circā adv., around
cīvis,cīvis m., citizen
cīvitās,cīvitātis f., state
clārus,-a,-um clear/famous
coepī,coepisse,coeptum (defective verb) began
cōgitō (1) to think/understand/consider
cognōscō,-nōscere,-nōvī,-nitum to recognize/know
committō,-mittere,-mīsī,-missum to commit/entrust
commūnis,-e common
comprehendō,-hendere,-hendī,-hēnsum to arrest/comprehend/understand
cōnferō,-ferre,-tulī,collātum to bring together/compare; **se conferre** to betake oneself
cōnor,conāri,conātus sum to attempt
cōnsilium,-ī n., plan
constituo,-stituere,-stituī,-stitūtum to decide/draw up

contineō,-tinere,-tinuī,-tentum to contain/hold together
cōpia,-ae f., abundance/supply; pl., troops/supplies
cornū,-ūs n., horn
corpus,corporis n., body
crēdō,crēdere,crēdidī,crēditum to believe/trust
creō (1) to beget/make
culpa,-ae f., fault
culpō (1) to blame
cum + abl. with
cum + indicative verb when
cūnctor,cunctāri to delay
cupiditās,cupiditātis f., desire/passion/avarice
cupidus,-a,-um desirous
cupiō,cupere,cupīvī,cupītum to wish/desire
cūr why?
cūra,-ae f., care/anxiety
cūrō (1) to take care
currō,currere,cucurrī,cursum to run
dē + abl. about/from
dēbeō,dēbēre,dēbuī,debitum to ought/owe
dēfendō,-fendere,-fendī,-fēnsum to defend
deinde/dein adv., then
dēlectātiō,dēlectātiōnis f., pleasure/delight
dēleō,dēlēre,dēlēvī,dēlētum to destroy/delete/wipe out
dēlinquo,-linquere,-līquī,-lictum to fail/be wanting
Delphī,-ōrum m. pl., Delphi
dēnique adv., at last/finally
deus,-ī m., god
dīcō,dicere,dīxī,dictum to say/tell/speak
diēs,diēī m., day
difficilis,-e difficult
dīligō,dīligere,dīlēxī,dīlēctum to esteem
discēdō-cedere,-cessī,-cessum to go away/depart
discipulus,-ī m., student/learner/disciple
discō,discere,didicī to learn
dissimilis,-e unlike/different/dissimilar
diū adv., for a long time
dīves,dīvitis adj., wealthy
dīvitiae,dīivitiārum f. pl., wealth/riches
doceō,docēre,docuī,doctum to teach
dō,dare,dedī,datum to give
dolor,dolōris m., pain
domus,-us f., house/home
dōnum,-ī n., gift
dubitō (1) to hesitate/doubt
dūcō,dūcere,dūxī,ductum to lead/consider
dulcis,-e sweet/pleasant/agreeable
dum while
dūrus,-a,-um hard/harsh
dux,ducis m., leader
efficiō,efficere,effēcī,effectum to effect/bring about
ego,mei I
enim truly/certainly/for/in fact/indeed
eō,īre,iī,itum to go
equus,-ī m., horse
ergā + acc. prep. against
ergō adv., therefore
ēripiō,ēripere,ēripuī,ēreptum to rescue/take away
errō (1) to err/go astray
et and
etiam adv., even/also
etsī even if/although
ēveniō,ēvenīre,ēvēnī,eventum to turn out/result
ex (ē) + abl. away/out of
exemplar,exemplaris n., example/model
exercitus,-ūs m., army
expellō,expellere,expulī,expulsum to expel/drive out
experior,experīrī,expertus sum to experience/try/test
exspectō (1) to expect/await
facilis,-e easy/agreeable
faciō,facere,fēcī factum to make/do
factum,-ī n., deed
fāma,-ae f., fame/rumor
fateor,fatērī,fassus sum to confess
fātum,-ī n., fate
fēlix,fēlīcis happy/lucky
fēmina,-ae f., woman
ferē almost
ferō,ferre,tulī,lātum to carry/bear/endure/bring
festinō (1) to hasten
fīdēlis,-e faithful/loyal
fīdēs,-eī f., faith/trust
filia,-ae f., daughter
filius,-ī m., son
fīnis,-is m., end/limit/boundary; pl. territory
fīo,fierī,factus sum to be made/be done/become
fōrma,-ae f., shape/form/beauty
fortis,-e strong/brave
fortūna,-ae f., fortune/luck
frāter,frātris m., brother
frūctus,-ūs m., profit/fruit
fugiō,fugere,fūgī,fugitūrus to flee
gēns,gentis f., gens, clan
genus, generis n., class/kind
gerō,gerere,gessī,gestum to carry on/conduct/accomplish
glōria,-ae f., glory
gracilis,-e slender
Graecia,-ae f., Greece
Graecus,-a,-um Greek

gravis,-e heavy/serious/severe
habeō,habere,habuī,habitum to have/hold/possess
hīc adv., here
hic,haec,hoc this/the latter
historia,-ae f., story/history
homō,hominis m., human being/man
honor,honōris m., honor/office/esteem
hōra,-ae f., hour
hortor,hortārī,hortātus sum to urge/implore
hostis,-is m., enemy
hūmānus,-a,-um human
humilis,-e humble/lowly
iaciō,iacere,iēcī,iactum to throw/hurl
iam adv., now/already
ibi adv., there
īdem,eadem,idem the same
igitur therefore
ignis,-is m., fire
ignōscō,-nōscere,-nōvī,-nōtum + dat. to grant pardon to/ignore
ille,illa,illud that/the former
immo on the contrary
immortālis,-e immortal
imperium,-ī n., absolute power/command
imperō (1) + dat. to give orders to/command
in + acc. into/against
in + abl. in/on
incertus,-a,-um uncertain
incipiō,incipere,incēpī,inceptum to begin
incolō,incolere,incoluī to inhabit
inde thence/then
iniūstus,-a,-um unjust
inquit he says/said
īnsidiae,-ārum f. pl., plots/treachery
īnsula,-ae f., island
intellegō,intellegere,intellēxī,intellēctum to understand
inter + acc. prep., between/among
interficiō,interficere,interfēcī,interfectum to kill
inveniō,invenīre,invenī,inventum to discover (come upon)
ipse,ipsa,ipsum himself/herself/itself
īra,-ae f., anger
īrascor,īrāscī,īrātus sum to be angry
is,ea,id, he, she, it, this, that
iste,ista,istud such
ita adv., so/thus
Italia,-ae f., Italy
itaque and so
iter,itineris n., march/journey
iubeo,iubēre,iussī,iussum to order/command
iucundus,-a,-um pleasant
iūdicium,-ī n., judgment/decision/court
iungō,iungere,iūnxī,iūnctum to join
iūs iūrandum,iuris iurandi n., oath
iūs,iūris n., right/law
iustitia,-ae f., justice
iūstus,-a,-um just
iuvō,iuvāre,iūvī,iūtum to help/aid
lābor,labōris m., labor/task/effort
laudo (1) to praise
laus,laudis f., praise
legō,legere,lēgī,lēctum to read/choose
lente adv., slowly
levis,-e light/slight
lēx,lēgis f., law
līber,lībera,līberum free
liber,librī m., book
līberō (1) to free/liberate
lībertās,lībertātis f., liberty/freedom
licet,licēre,licuit 3rd impers., to be allowed/ permitted
littera,-ae f., letter of alphabet; pl., epistle/ literature
lītus,lītoris n., shore
loca,locōrum n. pl., region
locus,-ī m., place/passage in literature
longus,-a,-um long
loquor,loquī,locūtus sum to say/speak/tell
lūdus,-ī m., school/game
lūx,lūcis f., light
magister,magistrī m., teacher/master
magnus,-a,-um great
maiorēs,maiōrum m. pl., ancestors
mālō,mālle,māluī to prefer
malus,-a,-um bad/evil
manus,-ūs f., hand/handwriting/band of men
mare,maris n., sea
māter,mātris f., mother
mediocris,-e ordinary/mediocre
memoriā teneō to remember
memoria,-ae f., memory
mēns,mentis f., mind/thought
mereō,merere,meruī,meritum to deserve/earn
metus,-ūs m., fear
meus,-a,-um my
mīles,mīlitis m., soldier
miror,mirārī,mirātus sum to wonder/be astonished (deponent)
miser,misera,miserum wretched/miserable
mittō,mittere,mīsī,missum to send
modus,-ī m., model/mode/measure/bound
moneō,monere,monuī,monitum to advise/warn
mora,-ae f., delay

morior,morī,mortuus sum to die
mors,mortis f., death
mortālis,-e mortal
mortuus,-a,-um dead
mōs,mōris m., custom/habit; pl. character/morality
moveō,movēre,mōvī,mōtum to move/arouse
mox adv., soon
multus,-a,-um much/many
mundus,-ī m., world/universe
mūtō (1) to change/alter
nam for
narrō (1) to tell/narrate
nāscor,nāscī,nātus sum to be born
natio,nationis f., nation
nātūra,-ae f., nature
nauta,-ae m., sailor
nāvigō (1) to sail
navis,-is f., ship
nē + subjunctive verb negative conjunction
nē . . . quidem not . . . even
nec adv., not; **nec . . . nec** neither . . . nor
necesse indecl. adj., necessary
neglegō,-legere,-lēxī,-lēctum to neglect
negō (1) to deny
nēmō,nēminis no one/nobody
neque and not; **neque . . . neque** neither/nor
nesciō,nescīre,nescīvī,nescītum to not know
nihil nothing
nimis (also nimium) indecl. adj./adv., too much/excessively
nisi except/unless
nōlō,nōlle,nōluī to wish not/be unwilling/refuse
nōmen,nōminis n., name
nōn adv., not
nōn sōlum . . . sed etiam not only . . . but also
nōndum adv., not yet
nōs,nostrum we
nosco,noscere,novi,notum to recognize/know
noster,-tra,-trum our
novus,-a,-um new
nox,noctis f., night
nūbēs,nūbis f., cloud
nūllus,-a,-um none/no
numerus,-ī m., number
numquam adv., never
nunc adv., now
nūntiō (1) to report/announce
ob + acc. on account of
obtineō,-tinēre,-tinuī,-tentum to hold/possess/obtain
occāsiō,occāsiōnis f., opportunity/occasion
occīdō,-cīdere,-cīdī,-cīsum to cut down/strike down/kill
oculus,-ī m., eye
odium,-ī n., hatred
offerō,offerre,obtulī,oblātum to offer
officium,-ī n., duty/office
omnis,-e every; pl., all
opus,operis n., work/task/deed/accomplishment
ōra,-ae f., shore
ōrātor,ōrātōris m., orator
orior,orīrī,ortus sum to arise
ōrō (1) to beg/entreat/beseech
ostendō,ostendere,ostendī,ostentum to show/exhibit
ōtium,-ī n., leisure
parcō,parcere,pepercī + dat. to be lenient to/sparing
parō (1) to obtain/prepare
pār,paris equal
pars,partis f., part/share
parvus,-a,-um small
patefaciō,-facere,-fēcī,-factum to open/throw open/lay open
pater,patris m., father
patior,patī,passus sum to endure
patria,-ae f., fatherland/country
paucī,-ae,-a few
pauper,pauperis m., pauper/poor man
pāx,pācis f., peace
pecūnia,-ae f., money
pellō,pellere,pepulī,pulsum to beat/strike
per + acc. through
pereō,perīre,periī,peritum to pass away/perish
periculum,-ī n., danger
perpetuus,-a,-um perpetual/continuous
persuādeō,-suādēre,-suāsī,-suāsum + dat. to persuade
peto,petere,petīvī,petītum to seek/petition
philosophia,-ae f., philosophy
placeō,placēre,placuī,placitum + dat. to be pleasing to
poena,-ae f., penalty/punishment
poēta,-ae m., poet
pōnō,pōnere,posuī,positum to put/place
populus,-ī m., people/nation
porta,-ae f., gate
possum,posse,potuī to be able
post + acc. after
praestō,-stāre,-stitī,-stitum to excel/exhibit/supply
praeteritus,-a,-um past
premō,premere,pressī,pressum to press/pursue/press hard

prīvō (1) to deprive
prō + abl. for/instead of/in front of
proficiscor,proficiscī,profectus sum to set out
propter + acc. on account of/because of
puella,-ae f., girl
puer,-ī m., boy
pugnō (1) to fight
pulcher,pulchra,pulchrum beautiful/handsome
putō (1) to think/imagine/suppose/judge
quaerō,quaerere,quaesīvī,quaesītum to seek/ask/ inquire
quam adv., how
quam than; + **superlative** as . . . as possible
quantus,-a,-um how large/how great/how much
quasi as if
-que enclitic, and
quī?quae?quod? adj., which? what?
quī,quae,quod who/which/that (relative pronoun)
quia because
quīdam,quaedam,quiddam someone/something/a certain one/a certain thing
quidem indeed/certainly
quis? quid? who? what? (interrogative pronoun)
quisque,quidque each one/each thing
quod because
quōmodo adv., how
quondam adv., once
quoniam since
quoque adv., also/too
rapiō,rapere,rapuī,raptum to seize/carry away/ snatch
ratiō,ratiōnis f., reason/judgment
recipiō,-cipere,-cēpī,-ceptum to receive/regain
redeō,redīre,rediī,reditum to go back/return
relinquo,relinquere,relīquī,relictum to relinquish/ abandon/leave
(re)maneō,-manēre,-mānsī,-mānsum to remain/ stay behind
remedium, -ī n., remedy
reperiō,reperīre,repperī,repertum to discover
requiēscō,requiēscere,requiēvī,requiētum to rest/ repose
rēs,reī f., thing
rēs pūblica,reī publicae f., republic
respondeō,respondēre,respondī,responsum to respond
rēx,rēgis m., king
rīdeō,rīdēre,rīsī,rīsum to laugh
rogō (1) to ask
Rōma,-ae f., Rome
Rōmānus,-a,-um Roman
saepe often
salveō,salvēre to be in good health
sapiēns,sapientis wise man/philosopher; adj. wise
sapientia,-ae f., wisdom
satis indecl. noun/adv., enough
scelus,sceleris n., crime/sin
scientia,-ae f., knowledge
sciō,scīre,scīvī,scītum to know
scribō,scribere,scrīpsī,scrīptum to write
sed but
semper adv., always
senātus,-ūs m., the Senate
senectūs,senectūtis f., old age
senex,senis adj./noun old
sēnsus,-ūs m., sense/feeling
sententia,-ae f., feeling/thought/opinion
sentiō,sentīre,sēnsī,sēnsum to feel/perceive/think
sequor,sequī,secūtus sum to follow
servō (1) to save/protect/preserve
servus,-ī m., slave
sī if
sī quis/sī quid indef. pronoun, anyone/anything
sīc adv., so/thus
signum,-ī n., sign/seal
similis,-e similar
sine + abl. without
sōl,sōlis m., sun
sōlus,-a,-um alone/only
soror,sorōris f., sister
spērō (1) to hope
spēs,-eī f., hope
stēlla,-ae f., star
stō,stāre,stetī,statum to stand/stand firm
studeō,studēre,studuī + dat. to be eager for/study
studium,-ī n., study/eagerness
stultus,-a,-um foolish
sub + acc. under (sub terram)
sub + abl. under (sub rege)
subitō adv., immediately
subitus,-a,-um sudden
suī reflexive pronoun, himself/herself/itself/ themselves
sum,esse,fuī,futūrus to be
superō (1) to overcome/surpass
superus,-a,-um above/higher
suscipiō,suscipere,suscēpī,susceptum to undertake
suus,-a,-um adj., his own/her own/its own
Syrācūsae,- ārum f. pl., Syracuse
tamen conj., nevertheless
tam adv., so/to such a degree
tandem adv., finally/at last
tantus,-a,-um so great/so much
telum,-i n., spear/weapon

tempestās,tempestātis f., storm/wind
tempus,temporis n., time
teneō,tenēre,tenuī,tentum to hold/possess
terra,-ae f., land
terreō,terrēre,terruī,territum to frighten/terrify
timeō,timēre,timuī to fear/to be afraid
tolerō (1) to tolerate/endure
tollō,tollere,sustulī,sublātum to raise/destroy/ lift up
tot adv., so many
tōtus,-a,-um whole/entire
trādō,trādere,trādidī,trāditum to hand down/ transmit
trahō,trahere,traxī,tractum to derive/draw/ drag/get
trāns + acc. across
tum adv., then
turpis,-e ugly/base/disgraceful
tū,tuī you (sing.)
tuus,-a,-um your (sing.)
tyrannus,-ī m., tyrant/absolute ruler
ubi when/where
ūllus,-a,-um any
umquam adv., ever
unde whence/from which
ūnus,-a,-um one
urbs,urbis f., city
ut + indicative verb as
uter,utra,utrum which (of two)
ūtor,ūtī,ūsus sum + abl. of means to benefit oneself by means of/use/enjoy
utrum . . . an whether . . . or
valeō,valēre,valuī,valitūrus to be strong
-ve or/nor (enclitic)
veniō,venīre,vēnī,ventum to come
verbum,-i n., word
veritās,veritātis f., truth
versus,-ūs m., verse/line
vertō,vertere,vertī,versum to turn
vērus,-a,-um true/real/proper
vester,-tra,-trum your (plural)
via,-ae f., way/road/street
victor,victōris m., victor
videō,vidēre,vīdī,vīsum to see/understand
vincō,vincere,vīcī,victum to conquer
vīnum,-ī n., wine
vir,-ī m., man
virgō,virginis f., virgin/maiden
virtūs,virtūtis f., courage/character/virtue
vīs,vīs f., force; pl., strength
vīta,-ae f., life
vitium,-ī n., vice/fault
vītō (1) to avoid/shun
vīvō,vivere,vīxī,vīctum to live
vocō (1) to call
volō,velle,voluī to wish/be willing
vōs,vestrum you (pl.)